The Secret Empire: The Hidden Truth Behind the Power Elite and the Knights of the New World Order

Dan Desmarques

Published by 22 Lions Publishing, 2020.

Table of Contents

Copyright Page. 1

Book Reviews. 3

Introduction. 5

Chapter 01: The Secret Alliances of The Knights Templar. 7

Chapter 02: The Global Empire of The Knights Templar. 11

Chapter 03: How The Knights Dominate Global Politics. 15

Chapter 04: How Secret Societies Control Governments. 19

Chapter 05: Why The CIA Assassinated Politicians. 21

Chapter 06: The Knights of The Tower and Sword. 23

Chapter 07: The Synergy of Global Interests. 25

Chapter 08: How the CIA Assassinated Politicians. 27

Chapter 09: The Rockefeller Family. 29

Chapter 10: How Secret Societies Appeared in Europe. 33

Chapter 11: The Secret Society of the Rose. 35

Chapter 12: The Great Secret of The Rosicrucians. 37

Chapter 13: The Beliefs of The Rosicrucians. 41

Chapter 14: The Purpose of The Secret Societies. 43

Chapter 15: The Knights of The Dark Side. 45

Chapter 16: Knights, Pirates and Nazis. 47

Chapter 17: The Secret Government. 51

Chapter 18: The Vatican Banking System. 55

Chapter 19: The Army of Satan.. 57

Chapter 20: History is Made with Betrayals... 59

Chapter 21: The Freemasons and the Jesuits. 63

Chapter 22: The Real American Dream. 67

Chapter 23: Never Trust The British! 69

Chapter 24: The Rothschild Family... 71

Chapter 25: The Empire of the Rothschild.. 75

Chapter 26: How Souls Are Bought and Possessed. 77

Chapter 27: Satanic Rituals and Human Sacrifices... 79

Chapter 28: Narcissism and Demonic Possession. 81

Chapter 29: The Branches of Neo-Occultism.. 83

Chapter 30: The Truth about Scientology and Psychiatry.................................. 87

Chapter 31: The Illusion Between All Religions. 91

Chapter 32: The Hidden Truth in All Religions.. 95

Chapter 33: The Spiritual and Sexual Perversions.. 97

Chapter 34: How Greed Corrupted the World. 99

Chapter 35: The Committee of 300 101

Copyright Page.

The Secret Empire: The Hidden Truth Behind the Power Elite and the Knights of the New World Order

By Dan Desmarques

Copyright © Dan Desmarques, 2012 (1st Ed.) All Rights Reserved.

Copyright © Dan Desmarques, 2014 (2nd Ed.) All Rights Reserved.

Copyright © Dan Desmarques, 2014 (3rd Ed.) All Rights Reserved.

Copyright © Dan Desmarques, 2015 (4th Ed.) All Rights Reserved.

Copyright © Dan Desmarques, 2020 (5th Ed.) All Rights Reserved.

Book Reviews.

These are some of the hundreds of positive reviews that the original version of this book has received since it was published for the first time:

- "It's an up and down rollercoaster! The book was a fascinating read. Very informative and educational." —Angel Blanco

- "Well written by a well-read individual. The information you will find here is priceless." —Kimber Wolfgang

- "This book was so enlightening. Please read it! It was sooo worth it! I am looking forward to reading more from this author." —Tamieya Turner

- "It is packed with very valuable information." —Nivek Redmond

- "There is some really good information in this book" —Alexander J. Everhart

- "Pretty awesome book! Well written." —Sylvester Stanley

- "I'm reading this book all the time. It is a great read" —Richard Palmer

Introduction.

The world keeps changing extremely fast, but either in times of abundance or scarcity, under persecution or with the control over mankind, many have prospered. And they did so by looking at the patterns of the world in which we live and with the understanding of such patterns.

At the top of this social hierarchy, warlords, totalitarian regimes, kings and queens, through their secret organizations, planned wars that changed the world in specific directions. And all of them claimed to do this in the name of their country, religion, God and even freedom.

However, their hierarchies led to the creation of secret societies but also secret governments and secret agendas, kept away from the general public and discussed in secrecy and in secret meetings. These secrets led to the accumulation of power in many realms of life. In fact, many of the greatest criminals in human history, remain alive and well to this day, still exercising positions of power and great influence in different countries.

This best selling book will show you the facts behind the real history of the world. For the first time ever, many conspiracies are connected and explained in a way that will challenge even the most willing believers. Because the truth is indeed more incredible than many would assume it to be.

This book has been in the best selling charts of Amazon for more than eight years in a row, although previously published under other titles, and there have been many attempts at removing it from the market, but if you found it, you are now presented with an unique opportunity to see what you were never taught in school or allowed to know.

The information presented here is based on a research that has taken more than twenty years to develop. And, for this reason, it resumes a vast amount of complexity in the best way possible.

The awakening that reading this book will cause you, will certainly lead you to a great moment of understanding in your life.

Chapter 01: The Secret Alliances of The Knights Templar.

Many of the current secret societies started in countries were the Templars went underground, protected by their kings, such as Scotland, Portugal and, later, due to a crisis in the crown of Portugal, also Spain — through what would be known as the Iberian Union, and which, ironically, brought forward the decline of Portugal from that moment onward.

The Portuguese would resent the spaniards until modern times over what occurred between the two territories in the past. And this, while up north, Great Britain was formed, taking advantage of the conflicts, to steal the lands once in possession of the two nations — the first true Global Empire.

History is always written by the winners, but nobody can deny the fact — proved again and again, through many historical events — that the British are nothing more than thieves, mass murderers and pirates. And could they have done things differently?

World maps and an immense technology on navigation — learned from the Arabs and Vikings, and brought to Portugal by the Knights Templar — as well as the monetary investments needed to put ambitious ideas into practice, had been already formed and tightly controlled. And the power of the Knights Templar was, at the time, in Portugal, which was, as well, their first nation. Portugal was destined to become the birthplace of their Global Empire.

The Portuguese are still unaware of the fact that their first King, D. Afonso Henriques, was not only the son of a Knight Templar but also a Knight Templar himself, trained by the Templars in the art of war and helped by the Templars to take the land — once known as Condado Portucalense — from the King of Spain, to make it the first and true Templar Nation. But why did the Templars choose this location among so many?

As documents of the period indicate, the original name of this land was Portugalia, i.e., the location from where the ships sale. The Templars were already prepared to shift their trading port from Venice to Portugalia, because they wanted to expand their riches and not remain constrained to the commerce in the mediterranean, which was becoming highly competitive and not as profitable anymore.

The only option for the British was to turn to piracy. But not only because the British lacked the resources and funds to pursue the same ends. Also because Portugal and Britain had formed an alliance in 1386 — The Treaty of Windsor — in which the two territories promised to help each other in times of war. They had formal obligations to help each other and not compete for the same resources.

This alliance served the Portuguese royal house countless times during the attempts of the Spaniards to conquer Portugal, but also during the Iberian Union, to break the two nations apart, in favor of the rebellious Portuguese faction who sough refuge and help in England. England would spearhead the Anglo-Spanish war on the side of the deposed Portuguese Royal House.

The reason for this strong alliance is self-evident in what was mentioned before. For both nations hided the descendants of the Knights Templar. And it is also for this same reason that, despite the fact that the treaty was only signed in 1386, the alliance had already been informally assumed since 1147.

In 1147, during the Siege of Lisbon, English and other northern European crusaders – en route to the Holy Land — stopped and helped the first Portuguese Kind — D. Afonso Henriques — conquer the city from the Moors. They were helping a companion of the army of the Templars in the same crusade.

The purpose of the Templars in Portugal was primordially to obtain the section of the European land in the hands of the Moors, and not only keep the territory independent from Spain.

The complete dependency and obedience of the Kings of Spain towards the Pope, made them a threat to the Knights Templar, as they could't trust the Spanish Monarchs.

THE SECRET EMPIRE: THE HIDDEN TRUTH BEHIND THE POWER ELITE AND THE KNIGHTS OF THE NEW WORLD ORDER

It is, however, ironic, that the Portuguese were eventually responsible for saving the Spanish Monarchy many decades later, when hiding their royal family in Estoril during the second world war. Or where they actually helping their own descendants?

Chapter 02: The Global Empire of The Knights Templar.

After the former Order of the Knights Templars in Europe was abolished, the Portuguese King Dinis, who refused to pursue and persecute the knights (who were basically his colleagues in the Order) changed the name of the Order to Christi Militia (Military Order of Christ), in order to maintain it, and while giving the impression that the Templars had vanished.

Not only was this possible, but the same King Dinis was also able to negotiate the recognition of this "New Order" with Clement's successor — John XXII — after Pope Clemente V mysteriously died in a fire, following a thunderstorm in which a lightening struck precisely the church where he was sleeping. The fire was so intense that, by the time it was extinguished, the Pope's body had been all but destroyed.

Was this a big coincidence or a payback from God on the Pope who betrayed the Knights Templar?

Probably both, considering that the Knights Templar were the CIA of medieval times.

The order survived and changed its plans, now heading to the sea with boats, and investing its treasure — previously accumulated from the protection service to kings (known today as an international banking system and an International Intelligence Service) — in the formation of the first Maritime Empire.

All the famous personalities behind the maritime explorations of Portugal were members of the Christi Militia, as their paintings, with the red cross on the chest, proves it. Among them, the most famous members of the Military Order of Christ were:

- Prince Henry the Navigator: Grand Master and son of King John;
- Manuel I: Grand Master and King of Portugal;

- Infante Ferdinand: Grand Master and King of Portugal;

- Sebastian of Portugal: Grand Master and King of Portugal.

Prince Henry is the pioneer of what would be formally known as the Age of Discovery. He was responsible for the early development of Portuguese exploration and maritime trade with other continents, through the systematic exploration of Western Africa, the islands of the Atlantic Ocean, and the search for new routes.

In other words, and contrary to what the Portuguese, themselves, are taught in school, their country didn't discover the unknown world. The Templars already had maps of the entire globe, including North and South America, as well as the wealth to build the boats which allowed the Portuguese and Spanish crowns to travel to vast lands.

This new strategy made Portugal the first and one of the richest global empires in history, far more than any other European nation at the time, including England, which was starving itself to death and too busy chopping heads of peasants who stole apples.

Piracy had to emerge out of the collective jealousy, poverty, hatred and greed of many European nations. And it was indeed piracy that brought the Portuguese Empire to its knees, by weakening it, as some of these nations also started attacking and stealing its trading ports in other continents.

The Portuguese had built ports for what would be the first world trading system and, basically, created the first World Trade Organization. But even though today we can say that they don't have the power they once had, it is interesting to notice that many occupy positions of influence in global affairs, and seem to be far more interested in world economics than the deplorable state of poverty in which their population is living.

As a matter of fact, until 2020, Portugal was still one of the countries with the widest gap between rich and poor inside the European Union, surpassed only by Bulgaria, Lithuania, Latvia and Spain. Portugal and Spain were only surpassed, in terms of inequality, by former Soviet Union states. Which means that they have always been more interested in world domination than their own development, or in giving equal opportunities to their own people.

The pride of the Portuguese and Spanish people on their history is delusional because the Elite of these nations never cared about their own citizens. The masses were used to serve the purposes of this Elite, just as what we have always seen in other nations and throughout history.

Chapter 03: How The Knights Dominate Global Politics.

The Order of Christ never vanished but rather infiltrated politics. We can see this when connecting the most prominent Portuguese figures of modern times, their place in world affairs, and the association they have with specific groups. So let us ponder on these coincidences for a moment:

- Antonio Guterres became the 9th Secretary-General of the United Nations and is a knight of the Order of Christ. The Portuguese Freemasons had this to say about him: "Portuguese Freemasonry congratulates António Guterres on his election as Secretary-General of the United Nations, and the fact he was unanimously acclaimed by the Security Council at the United Nations, which is an odd case in this organization. Freemasonry is now represented in the United Nations and at the ECOSOC (Economic and Social Council of the UN) by CLIPSAS (one of the largest Freemason Organizations), having its objectives aligned with what Universal Masonry has advocated for centuries" (In www.maconariaportugal.com).

In other words, they congratulated a fellow freemason, who happens to be also a knight of the Order of Christ. António Guterres is a Knight Templar leading the United Nations.

Another famous Portuguese, who is a knight of the Order of Christ with access to a position of influence in global affairs, is Jose Manuel Barroso:

- Former President of the European Commission;

- Chairman of Goldman Sachs International;

- Chairman of the Steering Committee of the Bilderberg Meetings;

- Knight of the Order of Malta.

Jose Manual Barroso replaced another knight of the Order of Christ, as the Chairman of the Steering Comittee of the Bilderberg Meetings: Francisco Pinto Balsemão.

Francisco Pinto Balsemão is...

- Chairman of the European Publishers Council;

- Founder of the first Portuguese Private Television Network (which he entitled "SIC");

- Member of the Portuguese Council of State;

- Freemason, from the Grand Orient Lusitano Lodge.

Francisco Pinto Balsemão participated in more than thirty conferences of the Bilderberg Group since 1981 — the same year in which he became the Prime Minister of Portugal and Minister of Social Affairs.

Balsemão replaced the Portuguese Prime Minister Francisco Sá Carneiro, whose plane crashed soon after takeoff from Lisbon Airport, in what was already confirmed to be a professional assassination — similar to the assassination of John F. Kennedy, and conducted by the same organization: The United States Central Intelligence Agency (CIA).

The association of secret societies with politics and terrorism has been seen publicly multiple times, namely, in 2003 — in the Azores Emergency Summit on War Against Iraq. A summit represented by:

- George Bush: Knight of the Skulls and Bones;

- José Manuel Barroso: Knight of Malta and of the Order of Christ;

- Tony Blair: Freemason;

- José María Aznar: Member of the Opus Dei.

THE SECRET EMPIRE: THE HIDDEN TRUTH BEHIND THE POWER ELITE AND THE KNIGHTS OF THE NEW WORLD ORDER

In resume, the NATO coalition against Iraq was formed by knights of different branches.

This was indeed a war that had nothing to do with weapons of mass destruction, reason why they were never found. This was a Holy War or, at least, a "Oily War", backed by the military descendants of the knights.

Chapter 04: How Secret Societies Control Governments.

The knights would never be stopped in their attempts to control the whole world.

In 1980, a small private aircraft carrying Portuguese Prime Minister Francisco de Sá Carneiro and Defense Minister Adelino Amaro da Costa crashed in Lisbon, Portugal. And even though initial investigations concluded that it was an accident, later parliamentary investigations found evidence of a bomb beneath the cockpit. After the Portuguese 15-year statute of limitations took effect, several people came forward confessing involvement in the crime.

Why would the Portuguese murder their own Prime Minister and Minister of Defense, as they were democratically elected and following decades of dictatorship, as well as a provisional military government?

It is exactly in this succession of events that the answer is found. For this was supposed to be the first democratically elected Portuguese Prime Minister, following the 1974 Carnation Revolution in Portugal.

These politicians opposed the conspiracy that they found going on behind their backs, just as John F. Kennedy did. And they faced the same fate and for the same reasons, and were murdered by the same people too. Such people were helping put in power Ronald Reagan, who was a Knight of Malta and a strong supporter of Freemasonry.

In other words, both the Freemasons and the Knights of Malta were behind these decisions, and received the support needed from the Military Order of Christ, which was involved in politics, the military or the secret services.

Between the Portuguese Revolution of 1974 and 1981, Portugal was ruled by a succession of Generals and other members of the revolutionary forces, who were involved in the arms trafficking between the United States and both the African and Middle-East Revolutionary Forces, through the Islands of Azores — a strategic point on the map for the U.S. Air Force to make the transportation. The purpose was a regime change in both African Nations and Arabic Nations, and which would favor the American Corporations led by the Rockefeller family.

These, supposedly, wars and revolutions for people's freedom, would lead to the establishment of dictatorships — conducted by students' movements, religious movements or communist movements, carefully orchestrated by the CIA.

Despite these facts, the majority of the Portuguese population truly believes, to this day, that their revolution was an inside job, intending to end the wars between Portugal and its colonies — a revolution in the name of freedom.

In truth, it was a conspiracy against Portugal conducted by its own corrupt military forces and with the aid of the American Secret Services.

Chapter 05: Why The CIA Assassinated Politicians.

In 1980, December the 4th, the Portuguese Prime Minister, Francisco de Sá Carneiro, was traveling with the Defense Minister, Adelino Amaro da Costa, who had said he had documents related to the October surprise conspiracy theory, and was planning on taking them to the United Nations General Assembly.

The October Surprise conspiracy theory refers to a plot to influence the outcome of the 1980 United States presidential election, contested between Jimmy Carter and his opponent, Ronald Reagan. At the time, one of the leading national issues was the release of 66 Americans being held hostage in Iran, and following their revolution, which was orchestrated by the CIA. The CIA had then conspired with representatives of Reagan's presidential campaign and Iran to delay the release until after the election, to thwart President Carter from pulling off an "October surprise", i.e, a news event which would influence the outcome of the US elections — the release of the hostages.

Once Reagan won the election, the Islamic Republic of Iran announced the release of the hostages almost immediately.

As a result, Reagan Administration and the CIA subsequently rewarded Iran for its participation in the plot, by supplying Iran with weapons and by unblocking Iranian government monetary assets in U.S. banks. In doing this, the United States were responsible for placing Radical Islamics in power, while helping overthrow the last of the Iran's monarchies — The Pahlavi Dynasty.

The last Shah of Iran, Mohammad Reza Pahlavi, was trying to keep his country free from both political and religious oppression, which infuriated the clergy, leading to several attempts on his life, and finally a national revolution with the aid of the CIA.

This revolution was orchestrated because, in march 1974, the Shah of Iran announced the intent of quadrupling the oil price in order to introduce a new order, more in line with the realities of the international community and the requirements of its development. In an interview for Tehran Radio, the Shah declared that, "As far as the industrial world is concerned, the era of extraordinary progress and income based on cheap oil has ended".

The Shah then reinforced this purpose in another interview, with Peter Snow, by saying that, "In 25 years, Iran will be one of the world's five most flourishing and prosperous nations of the world".

When asked about his opinion on western economy, he said the following:

"You do not work enough, you try to and receive more money than necessary for what little you do, and this situation cannot continue; it can possibly continue for a few months or for a year or two but not forever."

When challenged over the issue of democratization, the Shah was even more explicit, by answering with the following question:

"Who says the people of Iran want to have the type of democracy that you have in Britain?"

As the people of Iran were not interested in being democratized, this weakness was seized upon as an opportunity to enslave them with religious oppression. During the reign of the Shah, Iran had benefited from a very western lifestyle — women didn't have to cover their face, and there was an equality of opportunities in the country. The severe religious laws and the discrimination imposed by the oppressive Islamic regime that followed was the result of such revolution.

Chapter 06: The Knights of The Tower and Sword.

Apart from the documents that the Portuguese Minister of Defense had in his possession, and that could influence the Presidential Elections in the US, he also insisted in investigating the arms trafficking, which involved not only important American names but also the highest-ranks of the Portuguese Military.

It is important to mention that, contrary to popular belief, the Portuguese armed forces didn't replace any dictatorship with a *coup d'état* but rather were responsible for the transition between governments, since they themselves placed Antonio De Oliveira De Salazar (the dictator who ruled Portugal during the time of Hitler) in power, and following another *coup d'état* — in 28 May 1926 — intended to put an end to the Portuguese First Republic.

In essence, the Portuguese military created the dictatorship that the Portuguese suffered for nearly five decades and then ended it themselves. But why would they do it? To end the profitable wars in which they themselves participated?

The Portuguese Generals who took power in the leadership of the country, during the period of transition between what was supposed to be a democracy and the former dictatorship — under Antonio De Oliveira Salazar (a Portuguese Knight of the Order of the Tower and Sword) — where the following:

- António De Spínola, Knight of the Order of the Tower and Sword;

- Francisco Da Costa Gomes, Knight of the Order of the Tower and Sword;

- António Ramalho Eanes, Knight of the Order of the Tower and Sword.

As we can see, both the dictator placed in power by the arm forces and the generals who ruled the country before the transition to a "democracy", were all knights of the Order of the Tower and Sword. And, according to historian, freemason and professor, António Ventura, all these men were also selected by the Portuguese Lodges of Freemasonry.

This means that Freemasonry and the Knights of the Tower and Sword, both followed the same guidelines, and both would have to be involved in the arms trafficking. In fact, these generals were indeed accused by former CIA agent, Oswald Le Winter of helping in the arms trafficking, namely, Francisco da Costa Gomes — in the trafficking with Iran.

This succession of generals ended only with Mário Soares, a very popular Portuguese politician and communist, follower of the ideology of Karl Marx.

The Portuguese people loved him and truly believed he represented democracy and freedom. But that wasn't the case. Mario Soares was a traitor and also:

- Knight of the Order of the Tower and Sword;
- Knight of the Order of Christ;
- Freemason.

Since the end of the Portuguese Monarchy, the Portuguese people have been lied about the true history of their country. For as we can see here, they have always been ruled by the knights of the Tower and Sword under the supervision of Freemasonry, i.e., the British Empire. Portuguese Democracy is, in essence, an illusion controlled by the British through the lodges of freemasonry.

Chapter 07: The Synergy of Global Interests

Mario Soares was a criminal, a thief, a freemason, a knight of the Order of Christ, a knight of the Tower and Sword, a CIA agent and a politician, proving that this combination is indeed possible, and these Orders and Organizations are controlled by hypocrites without any integrity.

In an article published by the Portuguese newspaper 'Direita Política', it is said that Mario Soares is guilty of the "Genocide of the Portuguese living in Angola, money laundering and corrupt deals with the CIA, exchange of Portuguese territories for personal gain, theft and traffic of diamonds, drugs and ivory from Angola."

Oswald Le Winter — CIA agent — confirmed this, by saying that, "Soares was an opportunist"; which was confirmed as well by Der Spiegel (in 1974) in regards to the genocide of the Portuguese in Angola. In this interview, Soares is reported to have said: "We will shoot our white colonizers if necessary."

Mario Soares was referring to the Portuguese habitants who resided in Angola at the time of the decolonization — entire families who were slaughtered by the rebel armed forces.

He then reinforced the same beliefs in an interview to a Brazilian Journal (Estado de S. Paulo) in which he stated that the Portuguese residing in the former Portuguese colonies should be, in his own words, "Thrown to the sharks".

These crimes, which Mario Soares — Portuguese Prime Minister from 1983 to 1985, and President from 1986 to 1996 — formally supported against his own people, were paid by the CIA. In 2013, a Dutch TV Network (VPRO) showed a documentary in which the cycle of money of Mario Soares was exposed, as coming directly from the CIA in the United States and the Chinese Mafia — through the the Portuguese former colony of Macau.

Former CIA agent, Frank Carlucci, was one of Mario Soares friends, who helped him overthrow the Portuguese government and replace it with a corrupt government invested in the interests of the North American Power Elite, namely, the Rockefeller Oil Corporations. As a consequence, Mário Soares had to be a direct supporter of the corrupt government of Eduardo dos Santos — President of Angola for 38 years.

The opposition of Eduardo dos Santos was eliminated with the help of the CIA. And during the period in which Mario Soares and Eduardo dos Santos were in power, the son of Soares — João Soares — was responsible for the traffic of drugs, diamonds and ivory between these countries.

João Soares, who is still a famous Portuguese politician to this day, was free to enter the Portuguese territory with political immunity, using a private plane for this criminal activity. This was confirmed by Colonel Breytenbach, who said: "I discovered a mafia that smuggled elephant teeth and rhino horns, diamonds, wood and drugs. 100,000 elephants were killed to help finance the war."

The mafias would then take the ivory to Hong Kong and the diamonds to Pretoria, in South Africa, and Europe, through different transport companies.

Mário Soares and his son, João Soares, were never arrested or persecuted for any crime.

In 1995, João Soares became the Mayor of Lisbon, and later, in 2015, the Portuguese Minister of Culture. João Soares also publicly admitted to be a freemason since 1974, which means he joined when he was only 25 years old.

Apparently, both father and son, where freemasons, socialists and criminals, which means that the promise that the freemasons make upon joining the organization, of protecting each other in any given moment, also means that, in this case, they help each other in hiding horrific crimes.

Chapter 08: How the CIA Assassinated Politicians.

The global network of secrecy has been for many decades associated with the military, the secret services, politics, secret societies, terrorism and the mafia.

In 2012, Fernando Farinha Simões and José Esteves, claimed to have been paid $750,000 by CIA agent Frank Sturgis to create a bomb, which, according to them, was only an incendiary device, meant to scare the Portuguese Ministers (Francisco de Sá Carneiro and Adelino Amaro da Costa) into withdrawing from their intention of exposing the cabal and not to truly kill them. But they were, apparently, used as scapegoats, just as Lee Harvey Oswald, in the assassination of John F. Kennedy.

Feeling betrayed, they decided to expose the whole assassination plot. According to them, the CIA planted the real explosives that would turn the plane into a ball of fire — as many witnesses recall seeing that night —, even though it was denied by the Portuguese Secret Service, in an attempt to portray the crash as a mechanical failure.

The same strategy was used to murder the President of the United Staes — John F. Kennedy.

The fatal shots to the head of the President came from his own driver — William Robert Greer. And there is footage to prove this, even though it has been kept away from the general public. The footage was revealed by Milton William Cooper, who was also murdered by the CIA for exposing too much information that they didn't want the general public to know.

It doesn't take much research to realize that the ones behind the coverups are the same behind the murders. For the fake report on the death of President John F. Kennedy was conducted by the Rockefeller Commission Analysis. Yes, the same Rockefellers that promote revolutions through the CIA, and control the arm trafficking with the intent of overthrowing governments, to then replace them with corrupt leaders that favor their own private interests in the oil industry, as was with the cases of Portugal and Iran.

The United States President's Commission on CIA Activities within the United States, was set up under President Gerald Ford in 1975 to investigate the activities of the Central Intelligence Agency and other intelligence agencies within the United States.

In other words, the founder of this Commission — who would then become the 41st Vice-President of the United States —, Nelson Rockefeller, set up this commission in order to hide any crime perpetrated by the Intelligence Agencies.

In doing this, he could use them to freely perpetrate crimes in the name of his own family, as was with the case of John F. Kennedy.

Chapter 09: The Rockefeller Family.

The Rockefeller family descends from John D. Rockefeller, and are heirs to the monopoly of the oil industry in the Untied States. As such, they have interests in making special agreements with leaders who favor their investments in the oil market, and also the resources for that, through carefully orchestrated revolutions.

The revolutions and crimes conducted by the CIA are then hidden by the Institutions created by the Rockefeller.

These operations occur worldwide. In fact, in the Portuguese reports, it was mentioned that Frank Sturgis, who orchestrated the death of the Portuguese politicians, was also one of the CIA agents involved in the murder of John F. Kennedy, in Dallas, in the 22 of November 1963. According to the information provided, the bombs were placed in the plane by CIA agents freely moving around in the airport and in cars of the American Embassy.

In the day of the assassination of the Portuguese politicians, Frank Sturgis had a remote control in his hands, which he pressed to activate the bomb. And that's when the explosion occurred.

Following this public confession, Fernando Farinha Simões was then forced into a psychiatric institution, in an attempt to silence him. And yet, interestingly, before that, Simões had been invited several times by the TV Channel Network SIC (Owned by Francisco Pinto Balsemão — Chairman of the Steering Comittee of the Bilderberg Meeting, Freemason and Knight of the Order of Christ) to help spread lies related to the crime and make it seem as if it was an accident.

The same strategy was used in the United States, when the driver of John F. Kennedy was invited to talk on national television and lie about his own crime.

Even more interesting, is that one of the Portuguese TV shows to which the suspect was invited, was called "The Machine of Truth", and in which the participants had to answer questions through a lie detector. It was staged on camera! Not only was the Portuguese Police and the Military hiding the crime, but also the mainstream media, the reporters and the TV presenters.

Everything that happens in the world is well-planed, because many of the most influential knights, freemasons, generals, politicians and bankers, regularly meet to discuss their strategies in secret meetings. These meetings have many names but the groups where all founded by the same Rockefeller family:

- The Committee of 300;
- The Bilderberg Meetings;
- The Trilateral Commission;
- The Club of Rome.

These are illegal encounters, where a parallel government forms a synergy of purposes and interests, and in which the future of mankind is discussed far from the public eye.

Apparently, in their own view, the rest of the world has no right to know what they are planning in secret.

This level of worldwide coordination, conspiracy and terrorism, was never before seen or possible. For the first time, many secret orders, monarchies and organizations, as well as the Vatican, are united and acting towards the same agenda — the New World Order. But this is not a spiritual or religious world order. There is no moral, love or compassion behind it. The members are openly atheists.

The main goal of their encounters, as several leaked documents show, is a complete enslavement of mankind, while they get rich beyond measure and for many generations to come, forming a new global monarchy.

They also want to destroy the middle class and small business owners, so that they may be worshipped as gods by everyone and with absolute control. After all, these people are obsessed with power and secrecy like any other narcissistic psychopath, and that's what narcissists truly want — to be worshipped by the people they suppress, gaslight and poison.

Chapter 10: How Secret Societies Appeared in Europe.

As we can see by many world events, there's a strict coordination between freemasonry and orders of knighthood. And this happens because both share similar values. But in order for us to understand the relation between Freemasonry and the Knights Templar, for example, and which, as mentioned before, is indirect rather than direct, we need to first analyze the context of the time.

It is here that we find the correlation between those two groups and others, not so well-known, namely, the Cathars, the Gnostics, the Jesuits, the Rosicrucians, and the Sufi, among many other and smaller groups, and from a field that today is categorized as Wicca.

All of these groups were viewed by the nobility of medieval times as having a scientific and pragmatic approach to life. The monarchs sought to educate themselves in the esoteric and mystic arts that were closer to them. And the reason for such need was self-evident by their position in society.

The ability to see forth into the future could, in many cases, decide the outcome of a battle and help calculate the risk of an investment. It was crucial for the nobles to gain such control in the most mathematical way possible and also train themselves in the esoteric sciences.

The need for formulas and structures, guided their curiosity towards cartomancy, chiromancy, numerology, and astrology, which became very popular and vastly disseminated throughout the royal houses of Europe.

The combination of these practices became known as Western Esotericism, and developed into what today is better known as the Occult or the New Age combined body of knowledge.

As these practices where prohibited by the Vatican and didn't need a specific set of religious rituals, the study of the esoteric sciences became a secrecy, and their groups, an Elitist Group of Secret Societies.

Among these secret societies, some became more famous than others, not necessarily because they presented a more advanced approach to the spiritual knowledge, but rather because they were more well-organized, committed and well-funded. Fundamentally, the richer a group was, the more likely it was to survive the challenges of the time. And this is why Rosicrucianism became so popular.

As the word indicates, Rosicrucianism is the Order of the Rose. But why a rose?

There are different explanations as to why a rose was chosen by the Rosicrucians, or as to why they have chosen such name to represent themselves. But the most logical explanation to assume, also due to the historical evidence and the location of the first Rosicrucians, is that, being the rose red, it was an obvious symbol, as well as representation, of the descendants of the Templars.

However, many Rosicrucians have claimed that the meaning of the red cross of the Knights Templar had nothing to do with christianity, but was instead a symbol of the five alchemical elements — fire, water, air, earth and ether (at the center). And this belief leads us to assume that the Rosicrucians founded the Templars, just like they founded the Freemasons.

Chapter 11: The Secret Society of the Rose.

The rose is a symbol of love and spiritual transmutation. Therefore, it is very likely that the meaning of the rose precedes the red cross of the templars, inspiring its creation, and not necessarily being selected after them.

The Pythagoreans, for example, used the symbol of the pentagram to identify themselves, and which contains the same alchemical meaning.

The shape of the pentagram can be found in many flowers. And again, we find here the reason as to why the Rosicrucians picked a flower, as the pentagram is another of the symbols that they identify themselves with, and for the same reasons mentioned — the Rosicrucians see themselves as heirs of the Pythagorean Brotherhood — the Brotherhood of Nature and the Alchemical Transmutations Achieved through the Understanding of Nature.

As the Knights Templar became the nobility of Portugal and Spain, they also saw the rose as the ideal symbol to represent their spiritual lineage. For a flower could also and easily be offered to another person, to invite this person to a secret meeting, discreetly, and even in front of others; or be at the door of where a secret encounter would take place.

The rose was the ideal way of connecting the members of these secret societies, while avoiding the preying eyes of the Catholic Church, especially during the Inquisition, which sought to eliminate any rivalry against the power of the Vatican.

Today, Rosicrucians keep the tradition of using flowers in their encounters and offering it to their members, although merely as a symbolic gesture.

Through the veil of secrecy, the Rosicrucians spread to other countries and then gave birth to new groups, among which appears Freemasonry.

The use of special handshakes and code phrases, rather than flowers, was the chosen method used by the freemasons to keep themselves secret.

Many freemasons may reject what I just described, but those within freemasonry who have investigated the past, know that there is absolutely no historical evidence linking freemasonry with the Templars. It is an interesting viewpoint that gives more meaning to their group, but not rooted in facts.

Thomas De Quincey, in his work titled, "Rosicrucians and Freemasonry" suggested that Freemasonry is probably an outgrowth of Rosicrucianism, confirming what German Professor, J.G. Buhle wrote in 1803.

It is possible to assume, nonetheless, that due to the historical relations between Portugal and England, there have always been secret societies in both countries sharing the same esoteric knowledge, especially after a section of the templars sough refuge in Scotland.

The Freemasons, however, as an independent and formal organization, would only appear much later, around the 17th century, and amidst a conglomerate of many other similar groups.

Chapter 12: The Great Secret of The Rosicrucians.

The Rosicrucians learned to veil their esoteric practices through christianity and catholicism, and continue to do so today. Modern Rosicrucianism looks very similar to any other christian congregation. But it is not! The truth within Rosicrucianism is so well-hidden that even the majority of the members can't see it. Only their leaders know it!

Rosicrucianism evolved as a very sophisticated form of religious practice, and also by learning and taking the best from the most abstract forms of representing esoteric practices found in the oriental religions. It became a religion of symbols, emotions and structures — an extremely abstract religion hidden under many layers.

The spiritual layers formed in Rosicrucianism are also what veiled its greatest mystery and greatest secret. For the Rosicrucians, knowingly or unknowingly, practice what is known as inter-dimensional telepathic communication.

They do so through different states of mind, which are perfected with the practice, usually developed in solitude.

Interestingly, the vast majority of the members never reach such state of mind, not even after many decades of an existence dedicated to the practice. And this is the reason why there is a tremendous resentment and jealousy between themselves.

Their tendency for loneliness isn't a requirement as much as it is a consequence of the many conflicts within the Order, all of which arising from what they vow to fight the most — their own ego.

On the other hand, and as they also admit, "the enemy is within the Order", meaning that "their enemy", or Satan, is constantly trying to use the ego of the members against themselves.

Beyond the inner-battle in Rosicrucianism, and that has external consequences (and can also last a lifetime), few reach the highest spiritual level. Those who can, develop the capacity to see beyond the spectrum of light, as it is perceived by common people.

They can then feel energy fields around them, gain premonitions, and even communicate with the dead.

The vast majority has no idea of what I am talking about, and many won't even believe what I just said to be true. They live in the same darkness that they attribute to the rest of society. But, as mentioned before, it is a religion veiled in many layers, hidden even from its own members. These layers, although categorized in levels, are not restricted to such levels.

The founders of Rosicrucianism built the Order in such a way, that any student can ascend faster than others, or not, depending on his own moral level, ethics, and inner practice. The judgement here is always left for the spiritual world to decide.

The Rosicrucian Brotherhood is often metaphorical explained as not belonging to this physical reality, and many rosicrucians wrongly assume that this is related to their difficulty in being part of the world, or a need for more antisocial practices, when in fact, it just means that the Rosicrucian Brotherhood is not visible within the spectrum of light reached by our physical eyes.

The Rosicrucian Brotherhood is, in truth, an Order of Spirits. And these spirits choose exactly who can receive the knowledge and who cannot.

The practice in Rosicrucianism is merely a preparation to receive such higher knowledge — a process which the Rosicrucians believe to have been taught by Christ himself and hidden by the Vatican in order to form a higher authority around the Pope — and which the first rosicrucians believed to be the antichrist.

These beliefs are confirmed by the manuscripts that the Knights Templar found in Jerusalem, and that compose the collection of gnostic writings prohibited by the Pope and excluded from the Bible.

What the Knights Templar found is also in line with the Nag Hammadi Library, namely, the belief that Jesus was married to Mary Magdalene, and that she represented his Church.

As the manuscripts show, "Jesus loved her more than the other disciples" (In The Gospel of Philip) and "more than the rest of the women" (In The Gospel of Mary), and said to her: "Mary, thou blessed one, who I will complete in all the mysteries" (The Pistis Sophia), because "I have given you authority over all things and Sons of Light" (The Sophia of Jesus Christ).

The "Sons of Light", the "Order of Spirits" and the "Rosicrucian Brotherhood", are the same entities.

Chapter 13: The Beliefs of The Rosicrucians.

It may seem that the Rosicrucian Orders have different levels, depending on which one we are referring to, when in reality they only possess two: Ignorance blinded by arrogance and wisdom provided by the spiritual world.

In other words, everyone is left in complete ignorance, for decades, maybe an entire lifetime, if they can't reach the ideal state of mind — enlightenment.

Most members remain at the first stage during their entire existence, even if they participate in all the meetings of their Order and pay the necessary fees. Reason why the leaders developed a, somehow, equalitarian approach to the knowledge. For anyone with a lesser experience can share his insights with the rest of the group, if he or she has been chosen by the spiritual world to reveal their message.

This message becomes evident when revealed by more than one person in the group. And that is how the greatest secrets are revealed within the order, even for those who shouldn't have them.

In resume, spiritualism is the main and the biggest secret behind Rosicrucianism. All the branches of spiritualism emerged from such experiences within the Rosicrucian Order.

On the other hand, as Rosicrucianism developed towards an individual practice, one's evolution inside the Order has more to do with a karmic path and a spiritual awakening, but from a personal viewpoint, on what regards the lessons that must be acquired. As such, It is perfectly possible that someone, with only a few months of practice, may be able to see a lot more than another with over forty years of experience in the Order. It is not very common for this to happen but possible, and does happen.

As mentioned before, it is a religion within another religion — a group within another group. And so, the exterior representation of the level of the members doesn't necessarily correspond to the true spiritual level of each one or even their physical age.

In this sense, the Rosicrucians are the real Illuminati, at least, from a philosophical and theoretical approach on the topic.

This philosophical belief says that Divine Light can't be obtained by force, but instead earned, through a genuine confrontation with the self, the eradication of the ego, and a continuous development of the soul towards higher levels of empathy and compassion.

This belief is in line with Buddhism, Taoism, and Hinduism, among other religions, reason why the Rosicrucians study many.

According to Rosicrucianism, the eradication of the ego is merely the first stage in the path to Enlightenment. The following stage consists in the study of the One Universal Truth, also known as "The Book of Nature", for corresponding with the Divine Proportions or Golden Ratio, and the Sacred Geometry of Life.

Enlightenment, as it is believed, shall follow those stages, when the individual is prepared to receive the wisdom of the "Brotherhood of Light" or "The Spirit World".

Many christians would be shocked to know this, but they do the same, when referring to the "Holy Spirit" or "Angels".

In this sense, the real Illuminati here are the "Blessed Ones" mentioned by Jesus — those to whom "all the mysteries" are revealed, as they were also revealed to Mary Magdalene.

Chapter 14: The Purpose of The Secret Societies.

Due to the reasons already mentioned, we can't expect someone, who is developing higher levels of compassion, to be cruel. And this is why we can't confuse these Illuminati with the self-proclaimed ones, who lead their conduct by greed and the obsession for power.

We also can't label all the Rosicrucians as being Enlightened, if most of them haven't overcome the power of their own ego, greed and jealousy.

We can only say that, as a spiritual and religious structure, Rosicrucianism offers one of the most direct paths towards enlightenment — the assimilation of a Higher and Divine Light, and all the Wisdom that comes from It in the process.

This path demands many necessary sacrifices. For it is here that you find the perfect separation between light and darkness.

Therefore, while psychosis leads one group towards sadism and the pleasures of hurting others, even by violent means, compassion does the exact opposite, and seeks to heal humanity through love. And this is the message that Christ passed on to his followers, and the reason why many Rosicrucians see themselves as the true christians, and within the lineage of the ancient gnostics.

One of the main conditions to join Rosicrucianism, even today, and that is aligned to what I just said, is related to the absence of any form of cruelty, against humans or animals, and to see the purification of the body as being aligned with the soul, reason why Rosicrucians are either vegetarian or vegan.

Another condition to join this Society, or at least, not be expelled from it, consists in not interfering in political issues or events, and to never practice any form of illegal activity in the world. And so, there are not many Rosicrucians on the planet, contrary to what we see in Freemasonry. Very few people are willing to live in such a way.

Among those who exist today, very few practice what I just said, and for this reason, we can deduct that they are a very strict minority among minorities.

It is also not difficult to see that, if these principles were strictly applied, you would have far less members, as only about one in each a hundred of them fits the criteria expected.

We can then deduct why the highest members of the Order, as well as the founders, believe that it has always been doomed to vanish, as what occurred with the Pythagorean Brotherhood.

These groups then become represented by some other and new Order, and this is why their own leaders and senior members, as in Freemasonry, want me to write these books. For when all these Societies disappear, only books like this one will allow forming a new and better Order within the same lineage.

All Orders follow a lineage of wisdom that is in the direct relation to the path leading to the Divine Light representing the One Truth — God.

It is the purpose of all secret societies that this Truth never dies.

Chapter 15: The Knights of The Dark Side.

The lineage of the Dark Knights is not in accordance to what was supposed to be the purpose of the Secret Societies — to bring the Light of God to the word.

The Illuminati of today are bringing darkness to humanity instead. Because these groups — most of which founded by Rosicrucians, as explained before — have been perverted by the Dark Forces.

From 1159 to 1314 — year in which the last Grand Master of the Knights Templar, Jacques de Molay was sentenced to burn alive at the stake — the city of Tomar, in Portugal, was the European headquarters of the Knights Templar. And once the persecution of the Knights Templar took place, the order simply and uniquely changed its name to Order of Christ — to give the impression that the Templars had vanished from Europe — while the cross of the Order of Christ — the exact same one of the Knights Templar — painted in every single Portuguese caravel, proves otherwise. And why would they change anything, if they needed the same boats and the kings of Portugal were all members of the Order?

The expansion continued from that moment onward. But the influence of the Knights Templar in Spain only begun in 1581, after a succession crisis forced the Portuguese nobility to gather in the Convent of Christ in Tomar and officially recognize Philip II of Spain as King.

That was the beginning of the Iberian Union, which lasted from 1581 to 1640 — a period of singularity between the Crowns of Portugal and Spain.

The dynasty ended up ruling over nearly the entire known world, from the Americas to Southeast Asia.

Having control over both countries made it easier for the Templars to expand their fortune and influence beyond the limits of Europe, and control almost the entire planet.

However, the Knights Templar were always at odds with the two other Christian military orders: The Knights Hospitaller and the Teutonic Knights.

Merely two years before the persecution of the Knights Templar, in 1305, Pope Clemente V, sent letters to both the Templar Grand Master Jacques De Molay and the Hospitaller Grand Master Fulk De Villaret, to discuss the possibility of merging the two Orders. But neither was amenable to the idea.

Pope Clement then persisted for an entire year, inviting both Grand Masters to France to discuss the matter. And De Molay arrived first in early 1307, while De Villaret was delayed for several months.

While waiting for Grand Master De Villaret, De Molay and Pope Clement discussed criminal charges that had been made two years prior to the meeting by an ousted Templar, and that were being discussed by King Philip IV of France and his ministers.

It was agreed upon that the charges were false. However, Clement sent the King of France a written request for assistance in the investigation. And, according to some historians, King Philip, who was already deeply in debt to the Templars from his war with the English, decided to seize upon the rumors for his own benefit.

It is believed that Pope Clement was pressured into taking action against the Order. But that wasn't the case. For both the Pope and the King were relatives and both would benefit financially from this treason against the Knights Templar.

At the dawn of Friday — the 13th of October 1307 — King Philip IV of France ordered De Molay and scores of other French Templars to be simultaneously arrested. And, by Papal Decree, the property of the Templars was transferred to the Knights Hospitaller (now the Order of Malta).

This story was portrayed in a very popular science fiction movie — Star Wars.

As usual, successful fiction stories tend to be based on historical truths. Because that is how they connect to the collective subconscious.

In this case, the Pope can be compared to the Sith Lord. The knights who joined him are the Knights of the Dark Side.

Chapter 16: Knights, Pirates and Nazis.

The army of surviving knights was composed by two groups:

- The Knights of the Order of St. John in Jerusalem — later becoming known as the Knights of Malta, for being granted ownership over the island;

- The Order of Brothers of the German House of Saint Mary in Jerusalem, also known as The Teutonic Knights, due to the fact that they were mostly composed by teutons — a germanic tribe originating in Scandinavia (Denmark, Norway and Sweden).

While the Teutonic Knights were mostly descendants of the Vikings, the Knights of Malta were exclusively composed by the aristocracy of France, England, Italy, Spain and Portugal. But mostly France.

In fact, the "Kings of France, and notably Louis XIV, not only allowed their subjects to join the Order, but actively encouraged them to do so, by granting privileges and diplomatic posts, and by giving commissions in their armed forces to Frenchmen who were Knights" (Paul Walden Bamford, In 'The Knights of Malta and the King of France').

On acceptance into the Order of Malta, they were sworn to celibacy, poverty and obedience. But those vows quickly eroded away and the order became more of an honorable men's club than chaste.

There were not many who lived up to those ideals. For many were very wealthy and the Knights' standoffish attitude towards the locals does not always seem to have applied when it came to temptations of the flesh.

The Order was complacent and corrupt, with little to do but scour the seas for any booty that could be seized.

The Order of Malta turned to piracy, while the Order of Teutonic Knights initiated numerous campaigns against both christian and pagan territories, including Poland and the Baltic Nations, in order to secure a bigger land for their own masters — The Holy Roman Empire and the Holy See.

In essence, the Knights of the Order of Malta became the pirates of the sea, while the Knights of the Teutonic Order became the pirates of the land.

After Holy Roman Emperor Maximilian abandoned his support to the Teutonic Order — due to an alliance with the King of Poland — the Teutonic Knights converted to Lutheranism (The Protestantism of Martin Luther), and the Grand Master, Albert of Brandenburg, became the first Duke of the Kingdom of Prussia (a territory that once included today's northern Germany, northern Poland, northern France, Lithuania, Latvia, Estonia and Kaliningrad).

During the reign of Frederick William II (1744 to 1797) — first King of Prussia — the nation practiced Enlightened Absolutism, and protected immigrants fleeing from religious persecution.

Prussia became a safe haven for anyone escaping the claws of the Vatican.

In 1871, the King of Prussia — Wilhelm I — would also become the first German Emperor. The Imperial German Army became, in practice, the Prussian army.

In the sequence of the German Revolution of 1918, Prussia proclaimed itself a Free State. The state of Prussia then became governed by a coalition led by several parties. But one party in particular — the Nazi Party of Adolf Hitler — gained more and more influence over time and a strong popular support due to its ideology.

The black eagle on white background used by the Nazi Party was, in facto, the coat of arms of the Teutonic Knights. And the Prussian monarchs quickly became supporters of the Nazi Ideology, which was also their ideology.

Eventually, all the nazis would have the black Teutonic Knight's cross on their uniforms, as a symbol of what they represented — the rebirth of the Teutonic Order of Knighthood.

This Teutonic Order never ended and continues to exist to this day, being ruled by a succession of Roman Catholic Priests — Grand Masters of the Order.

The Order is controlled by the Vatican since 1929, which means that it is a Roman Catholic Religious Order before the nazis even decided to associate with it. And for this reason, we can also say that the nazis where, at least in theory, an army of the Vatican.

The Grandmaster during this Inquisition was the priest Robert Johann Schälzky, from today's Czech Republic.

The Order served the Pope well, as it wasn't only the Jews that the Nazis persecuted, but also other non-catholic religions.

Chapter 17: The Secret Government.

The Portuguese and Spanish descendants of the Knights Templar — The Order of Christ — competed for maritime domain and eventually divided the world in two between themselves — in what would be known as the Treaty of Tordesillas, signed in 1494. But the Knights of Malta and the Teutonic Knights, formed a secret government, ruled the Vatican and the Holy Roman Empire (which lasted until 1806), competing in the shadows for the same world domination.

Their modus operandi was the same as it is today, and was perfectly described by John F. Kennedy in one of his most famous public speeches, when he said:

"We are opposed around the world by a monolithic and ruthless conspiracy that relies primarily on covert means for expanding its sphere of influence — on infiltration instead of invasion, on subversion instead of elections, on intimidation instead of free choice, on guerrillas by night instead of armies by day."

The medieval symbol of piracy became the skull and crossbones, because it replaces the white cross of the Knights of Malta, and it is actually a christian symbol as well. It derives from the Chi-Rho monogram, meaning Christos. It is the same symbol of the Skulls and Bones Society and literally means Knights of Christ.

The development of this Secret Government was always associated with power, control and the manipulation of the world economy. Murder, piracy and terrorism, was always, as we can see by our history, included in their actions.

"The ends justify the means" is a motto that could certainly be attributed to this society.

They would then work to recruit the brightest and most influential minds of the Academia, in order to fulfill their political goals.

The Skull and Bones Society, a branch of the Knights of Malta, has in the present day its headquarters in Yale University — Connecticut, United States — and prides itself of having among its most famous members well-known presidents:

- US President George H. W. Bush;
- US President George W. Bush (son of George H. W. Bush);
- US President William Howard Taft.

This Secret Government never entered our history books, because it is related to parallel and secret activities, and not official ones, between the same nations that had peace agreements between one another.

Even though the Portuguese (and later also Spanish) Order of Christ, descending directly from the Knights Templar, was able to accumulate a vast wealth in gold and silver, the Secret Society, composed by the Knights of Malta and the Teutonic Knights, took a different trajectory, by attacking the Portuguese and Spanish ships directly, and as well as their colonies.

As a matter of fact, Portugal and Spain, as catholic nations, were still being supervised by the Vatican, which meant that the Order of the Knights Templar had to be as discreet as possible, and even share the same space with priests and bishops who would report everything back to the Holy See, and in particular, the confessions of the christians, which were supposed to be confidential but never truly were.

This spying activity from the Vatican needed a secret agency to be more organized and well-coordinated, which led to the foundation of The Society of Jesus, also known as The Jesuits, in 1540.

The opening lines of the founding document declared clearly that the society was founded for "Whoever desires to serve as a soldier of God to strive especially for the defense and propagation of the faith and for the progress of souls in Christian life and doctrine".

This explains why the Jesuits are thus sometimes referred colloquially as "God's soldiers".

The Vatican had now three different militias at their disposal:

- The Knights of Malta — Sea Pirates;
- The Teutonic Knights — Land Pirates;
- The Jesuits — Secret Intelligence Agency.

Chapter 18: The Vatican Banking System.

The expansion and popularity of Western Esotericism, accompanied by many revolutionary ideas — in the fields of art, music and literature — gained sufficient influence to lead us to the age of enlightenment in 1715. However, this mass awakening made the Vatican loose a significant amount of power.

The Inquisition, and the condemnation of well-known public figures, such as Giordano Bruno, to be burned alive in pubic squares, in order to keep a tight control over the masses through fear, was clearly not enough.

The Vatican was losing control over nations that eventually turned to Protestantism and other religious faiths.

The tactic adopted to solve this problem was to create alliances that would turn European nations against one another. And this was done through The *Institutum pro Operibus Religionis* — The Vatican Banking System.

Gerald Posner, author of God's Bankers, says that, during World War II, the church had sizable investments and created the Vatican Bank in order to hide its financial dealings with the Nazis from the U.S. and the U.K..

"They abdicated their moral position as the head of the world's largest religion, especially at a time that they continued to make money with the people committing the murder. And bundled together life insurance policies of Jewish refugees who had been sent to Auschwitz and other death camps. They escheated these policies early on — meaning they took the cash value of them" (Gerald Posner).

Later, when the surviving children or grandchildren of the victims tried to collect on the insurance policies, they were refused.

This strategy never ended but rather expanded. In June 2013, the Italian police arrested a priest, named Monsignor Nunzio Scarano, with charges of fraud and corruption, together with a secret service agent and a financial broker. The three were caught attempting to smuggle €20M by private plane across the border to Switzerland.

The prosecutors alleged that they were using the Vatican Bank to transfer money from Naples — widely regarded in Italy as a haven of organized crime.

The Holy See naturally reacted to this as if they had no connection to the incident and were shocked by what screamed across the Italian press.

However, also in 2013, The Financial Times reported that the Deutsche Bank, JPMorgan and UniCredit, among dozens of others, including some of the world's biggest financial institutions, were for years "correspondent" banks to the Vatican, and moved as much as €2 billion a year from the Vatican's Bank to other bank accounts across the globe.

In one of its annual reports, it was verified that the Vatican Bank had 19,000 clients from around the world, 33,000 accounts and €5 billion in assets.

Half the bank's clients where religious orders: About 15% are Holy See institutions; 13% are cardinals, bishops and clergy; and 9% are from Catholic dioceses around the world. The rest of the clients of the Vatican are split among those who have, or should have, some "affiliation to the Catholic Church".

Vatican insiders also revealed that the bank is awash in donations and cash, from Sunday collections and charitable giving. As much as 25% of the bank's business is done in cash — a feature that regulators said raised red flags for money laundering.

Chapter 19: The Army of Satan.

The nazis never invaded countries that were subservient to the Pope, even though these nations claim to have been neutral during World War II, namely, Portugal, Spain and Switzerland.

In reality, Portugal and Spain were under the control of two catholic dictators who helped Hitler and his nazi associates escape to South America. And Switzerland kept all the gold and other artifacts that the nazis stole from the jews and other religious groups.

Not only the Vatican accumulated a vast amount of wealth through the nazis, but also got rid of many religions that were spread all over Europe and diminishing the authority of the Catholic Church.

Through many well-organized terrorist organizations and criminal activities, invested in the subversion of the established powers, and the promotion and financing of rebellious factions that supported the plans of the Vatican, a war between darkness and light would never end.

On one side, any spiritual evolution would be suppressed, ridiculed or furiously attacked. And on another side, there would be a need for secrecy to maintain this light hidden from the public eye.

The word Illuminati has been the source of much controversy and confusion because there are two Illuminati agendas — the hidden powers of the shadow government and the true God's army.

Both are the Illuminati, because one carries the light of God and the other carries the light of Lucifer. One group is attempting to promote spiritual freedom while the other wants to enslave mankind. One promotes a spiritual awakening while the other suppresses any information from entering the public spectrum.

These two armies — the knights of light and the knights of darkness — often cross paths, even inside their own organizations, institutions and religions.

Inside every religious group, you encounter distrust amidst the members, and a division between the imbeciles that follow blindly and those who understand the meaning of the universal truth and moral.

This situation occurs from the seemly open ones — like the various christian sects — to the most secretive — such as the Freemasons and the Rosicrucians.

The division is found as well in what concerns the topic of secrecy. Because while those at the bottom systematically insulted me, and told me to stop writing books like this one that you are reading right now, the leaders of Freemasonry, Rosicrucianism, Scientology, the Jehovah Witnesses, Buddhism, Mormonism, among dozens of many other groups, and that I have encountered personally, were happy to have me among them, and encouraged me to keep writing and spreading their wisdom.

In fact, my connections today with these groups, are all coming from the top, and not the bottom. I constantly receive books and messages from these members, helping me expand the Light to the rest of the world.

Chapter 20: History is Made with Betrayals.

Although this is not publicly admitted, many leaders of Secret Societies are perfectly aware that their groups have been corrupted and are doomed to end.

They also know that most of their members are in the darkness. The transition is obvious by the history of many other Orders:

- The Teutonic Knights, started as a militia that persecuted religious dissenters, later formed an empire that protected these same dissenters, and eventually merged with the nazis, to persecute in the name of the Vatican;

- The Knights of Malta, started as a militia composed by the nobility of the best families of Europe, and turned to piracy;

- The Knights Templar, protected christian history and artifacts, but later became corrupted by the Freemasons, a branch of their own creation.

The same we saw happening with nations, and how they betrayed each other. The Portuguese, for example, still believe that their greatest threat was Spain, and yet, they were betrayed, and tremendously, by their greatest ally — Britain.

The World Trade Organization — in practice founded by the Portuguese, through the Order of Christ — was stolen by The Rothschild and the Freemasons.

Nonetheless, we need to look deeper for the reasons, for they are rooted in greed and jealousy — a spiritual corruption influenced by the Dark Powers.

A good friend of mine, who was a leader in the Spanish Freemasonry (before he died at the age of 82), told me explicitly that the majority of the freemasons hate me due to jealousy. Because, by knowing too much, I have the power to ask the right questions and shift their Order too easily in a new direction.

In other words, they are a cult of lies, not truths. And these lies have nothing to do with Freemasonry as it was intended by their own founders. They fear consciousness at this point.

This was something that my friend warned me about, so that I may never be corrupted by their real intentions. He made it clear that the Lodges are independent, and there is darkness in most of them. Even though, they were happy to share my books and read them.

Another friend, leader in the Spanish Rosicrucian Order, told me: "Ignore the majority of the Rosicrucians, because they don't know what they speak."

He was warning me about the importance of writing these books and ignoring the many who opposed these revelations.

The same occurs inside the Catholic Church. Many catholic priests have opposed the Vatican, claiming that it houses the Devil. And one of them was the famous Irish exorcist Malachi Martin, who said (In an interview to Mr. Bernard Janzen of Triumph Communications, in 1990):

"There was this consecration, this enthronement of Satan within the Vatican, of Lucifer. It's a historical fact. It was done one particular day by a certain group of people representing Luciferians all over the world, especially American Luciferians. Therefore, in a certain sense, Lucifer has power. He doesn't own yet, but I'm sure he hopes to own some Pope as his man."

In his book, "Hostage to the Devil", one of the cases that Malachi Martin reports is related to a priest who was demonically possessed. According to him, demonically possession among priests is extremely common, which explains their perversions and scandals, namely, associated with pedophilia.

This contamination by the Dark Powers had been predicted by Jesus, when he said (In Acts 20):

THE SECRET EMPIRE: THE HIDDEN TRUTH BEHIND THE POWER ELITE AND THE KNIGHTS OF THE NEW WORLD ORDER

"Take heed to yourselves, and to the whole flock, wherein the Holy Ghost hath placed you bishops, to rule the church of God, which He hath purchased with His own blood. I know that, after my departure, ravening wolves will enter in among you, not sparing the flock. And of your own selves shall arise men speaking perverse things, to draw away disciples after them."

In essence, the Army of Lucifer was formed from within the religions and groups that have corrupted themselves over time. Their titles do not correspond to the intention of the founders anymore.

Lucifer took the different armies of Knights and the Holy See, along with all the religions in the world, and made himself Emperor. Lucifer is the ultimate ruler of this army of greedy narcissists and psychopaths. And, in hiding himself behind powers that appear to be noble and good, "The greatest trick the Devil ever pulled was convincing the world he didn't exist" (Charles Baudelaire).

This army is now occupying positions of power all over the globe.

Chapter 21: The Freemasons and the Jesuits.

The Vatican kept expanding its influence by enlisting famous criminal organizations in its ranks and by sponsoring wars against nations that opposed the Catholic Church in order to weaken them.

Among the many Secret Societies that joined this war, after being infiltrated by agents of the Vatican — The Jesuits — is Freemasonry.

The Stone Masons Society, or the Society of the Freemasons, was created by Rosicrucians, but became corrupted by the Vatican because they were often working for the Catholic Church, building cathedrals and churches, using the knowledge of sacred geometry passed unto them. It was easy to corrupt them because the church was too powerful and had a vast amount of wealth, especially during a period in which Britain was too weakened by financial problems.

This doesn't mean that the Freemasons are or were a criminal organization. But rather that they formed an alliance between themselves, the Vatican and the British Monarchy, in order to overthrow the Iberian Empire — formed by Portugal and Spain — and secure the financial interests of the members.

Many members of the Royal Family of Great Britain became freemasons, namely, King Edward VII, King Edward VIII and King George VI. But one of the greatest victories for this alliance, was the recruitment of the first Emperor of Brazil — The Portuguese, Pedro I.

In an open opposition to his father — King John VI of Portugal — Pedro, who was a Freemason, a Knight of the Order of Christ and a Knight of the Order of the Tower and Sword, did the same thing as the founding fathers of the United States (who were also freemasons) and proclaimed Brazil's Independence in 1820.

It was through Emperor Pedro that Freemasonry entered and expanded in Brazil, and the Vatican was then able to infiltrate and control the Brazilian Republic.

As a result, the first five Presidents of Brazil — Marechal Deodoro da Fonseca, Floriano Peixoto, Prudente de Morais, Campos Sales, and Rodrigues Alves, were all freemasons.

Brazil was a very important colony for the Portuguese Empire, and what Pedro did was an act of treason against his own country. By separating Brazil from Portugal, the exclusivity of the commerce between Europe and Brazil, going through Portugal — and that was keeping this nation as one of the wealthiest in Europe — came to an end.

This change enriched British business owners — many of whom were Freemasons — and consequently, the British Crown. Or, more precisely, the House of Rothschild, as they are the "Crown" of the British Monarchy.

Upon the death of his father, Pedro — The former Emperor of Brazil — would return to occupy the Portuguese throne as King Pedro IV, and face the consequences of his own acts. For after Portugal was weakened by another Freemason — Napoleon Bonaparte — who invaded the territory in 1807, the British seized the opportunity to colonize the country.

In an attempt to end the monarchy of Portugal and replace it with freemasons (that would establish a secret coalition through British Freemasonry), a clandestine Supreme Regenerative Council of Portugal was formed by army officers and freemasons, and headed by General Gomes Freire de Andrade — Grand Master of the Grande Oriente Lusitano Lodge and former General under Napoleon.

In order to avoid resistance, they promoted their intent as being the independence of the territory from both monarchic Influences — Portuguese and British.

That didn't stop followers of the monarchy from starting civil wars, which would eventually be led by Pedro, the former Emperor of Brazil.

Although he eventually won, his victory was short lived. And so was the victory for the Portuguese Royal House.

THE SECRET EMPIRE: THE HIDDEN TRUTH BEHIND THE POWER ELITE AND THE KNIGHTS OF THE NEW WORLD ORDER

In 1908, the Portuguese King and his elder son, and heir to the throne, were both shot in the same way as John F. Kennedy, when their chariot was crossing through a public square.

The youngest son — Manuel II, survived, and would be the last King of Portugal, after facing a civil war between the revolution army and the army of the monarchy.

The republicans finally won but, as historian Stanley Payne pointed out, "The majority of Republicans took the position that Catholicism was the number one enemy of individualist middle-class radicalism and should be completely broken as a source of influence in Portugal". As a result, a series of anti-catholic laws and decrees followed, and many Jesuits lost their citizenship, being forced to leave the territory.

The Vatican fought back with a *coup d'état*, headed by freemasons and knights of the Tower and Sword, and replaced this republic with a dictatorship that did the exact opposite for the next decades — unifying the power of the Vatican, the Freemasons and the Jesuits under the veil of a Portuguese Presidency — The dictatorship of António de Oliveira de Salazar.

The British had succeeded in ending the Portuguese Empire and transforming this territory into one of their many colonies, even though most of the population didn't even notice it occurring.

Some dissidents did try to orchestrate civil wars against the colonizers in power, but lost in their many attempts.

With the death of Manuel II, heir to the throne, and who was exiled in England (and was most likely murdered at the young age of 42), the hope for the reestablishment of the Portuguese monarchy died with him.

Chapter 22: The Real American Dream.

Even though nearly all religions were created with good moral intentions, they became corrupt by the influence of greed, and through those who could control such greed — The Vatican.

The groups that resisted these corrupt deals were either destroyed or financially starved to death. One way or another, through persecution or debt, they were all extinguished.

The only reason why some groups exist today and are allowed to prosper and expand, is because they favor the powers above them, while keeping everyone, all of their followers, in the darkness. For no religion today truly allows their members to reach for enlightenment, despite their claims and history.

What is also interesting here, is that these Secret Societies would eventually turn against their own masters, as was the case of the rebellion in the United States against the British Empire, and which was led by freemasons.

The United States Declaration of Independence is not only a declaration of independence from the monarchic powers of England, but also from the rulers in the shadow government and within Freemasonry.

The founders of the United States wanted a truly independent nation and a new territory, free from any type of oppression, either political, aristocratic, or religious. And this is what makes the Bill of Rights so important.

Those who wrote it were very aware of the methods used to control nations, and wanted to break away from this cycle. And, naturally, for this to occur, such territory would have to protect the freedom of speech and the right to bear arms.

In doing so, the freemasons divided themselves between an open fraternity in the United States, dedicated to a real enlightenment — as was intended by the founders of Freemasonry — and the corrupt and aristocratic freemasons of Great Britain, who were cooperating with the Vatican.

These freemasons were the true founders of the American Dream — the dream of freedom from persecution and control from the Elites. Reason why John F. Kennedy said: "We are as a people inherently and historically opposed to secret societies."

Notice that he mentioned a precise combination of two words — "historically opposed" — meaning that the United States were created to be a free and independent nation.

Many of the Lodges of Freemasonry in the United States have absolutely no link to any Lodge in Great Britain. They could even be considered non-masonic Lodges or illegal Lodges. And it was the need to be reconnected to the past, that allowed the corruption present in England to reenter the United States.

Today, the Masonic Lodges of the United States that are linked to British Lodges have been corrupted and no longer represent true masonry. But that would have to eventually occur, as at this point the British Empire was already global, after replacing the control of the Portuguese in the world trade business.

Chapter 23: Never Trust The British!

The cooperation that the Portuguese had with the Chinese, the Indian and the South African governments, through different ports, would soon be replaced by a brutal invasion and holocaust.

The words racism, barbarian and betrayal wouldn't have the emotional baggage that they have today, without the horrors that the world faced at the hands of the British Empire.

The constant lying, breaking off of agreements, and the assassination of innocents, including women and children, and politicians, was a common practice of this Empire and throughout their many colonies.

In fact, the concentration camps are an invention of the British Empire. They were used first in 1758 in North America, and had the name of Indian reservations.

After convincing, through deceptive agreements, or forcing, the Native Americans to enter such reservations, they would then be exterminated through starvation and biological warfare. And yes, biological warfare is also a British invention. It was used in 1763 for the first time, by giving blankets and other items contaminated with smallpox as gifts to the Native Americans.

The idea of offering death wrapped in gifts, offers and agreements, is also a very British thing to do. Their whole empire is based on such practices. So much so that we can question if the British Empire ever won a war that didn't imply betraying someone.

The refugee camps were again used in South Africa, in 1900, and with the same deception. They were presented as refugee camps, in order to deceive the local civilian families, who had been forced to abandon their homes for any reason which was related to the war.

Entire local families, including women and children, would then be exterminated in these camps through starvation.

The world should have learned its lessons and know that the British can't be trusted for absolutely anything. And yet, they continue to assume positions of leadership, despite being one of the most brutal and disgusting nations the world has ever seen.

History is always written by the victors, and yet, whoever is not very stupid, can see that the British Empire has been far more brutal than the Nazis ever were. It is, for sure, and clearly, the most racist in the history of empires.

It is the indoctrination of the educational system, that keeps the people of the United States, Portugal and Spain, among many other nations, blind to the massive betrayals received from the British.

Chapter 24: The Rothschild Family.

The expansion of the British Empire, with the help of Freemasonry, the Jesuits, the Order of Malta and the Vatican, led to the creation of the East India Company in 1600, and the first World Stock Market Exchange, to replace a monetary system based on gold and silver (which was at the time the basis of the Iberian Empire), later allowing Britain to gain control over the trade monopoly with interest backed by shares on paper, leading to the creation of paper-money as we see it today.

In essence, banknotes are worth nothing. Real money is still gold and silver. But by inventing the banknotes, the British Empire was able to substantially increase its investments, through what we know today as loans.

The East India Company (1600-1874), with headquarters in the United Kingdom, was owned by the Rothschild family. The same family who later set up the World Bank, the IMF and the Bank for International Settlements.

They also established an independent nation for themselves — The City of London — which is composed by a council of 12 board directors and a mayor.

The East India Company became the ruling power house in India. And by 1803, at the height of its rule, the British East India Company had a private army of about 260,000 — twice the size of the British Army.

"The Government of India Act of 1858 removed the Company as rulers of India, and the Company's armies, territories, property and powers passed to Crown rule" (In Rothschildarchive.org). But the word "Crown" refers here to the House of Rothschild — Crown of the Empire — and not the Monarchs of Great Britain. Therefore, in practice, the rulers remained the same.

The Rothschilds, due their achievements, were elevated to the title of Barons, by the last Holy Roman Emperor — Francis I — and then again in England — through the British branch of the family. Over the centuries, the Rothschilds then started to marry outside their own family, and usually into the aristocracy or other financial dynasties, to keep their supremacy.

The banking monopoly of the Rothschild family, in parallel with the Vatican, kept expanding and enriching both states — the Holy See and the City of London — allowing them to apply a more coercive control over governments, to change the fate of different nations, as was the case of Portugal and Spain. Both were now at the hands of the Vatican and the Rothschild family through their own Secret Societies and Orders of Chivalry.

In fact, "The Rothschild Family was directly involved in the independence of Brazil from Portugal in the early 19th century. Upon an agreement, the Brazilian government should pay a compensation of two million pounds sterling to the Kingdom of Portugal to accept Brazil's independence" (In Wikipedia.org/wiki/Rothschild_family).

Rothschild & Co (A multinational investment bank and financial services company), and the flagship of the Rothschild banking group, controlled by the French and British branches of the Rothschild family, was pre-eminent in raising this capital for the government of the newly formed Empire of Brazil on the London market.

Part of the price of Portuguese recognition of Brazilian independence, secured in 1825, was that Brazil should take over repayment of the principal and interest on a £1,500,000 loan made to the Portuguese government in 1823 by Rothschild & Co.

Now with the power to create and destroy entire nations, the Rothschild could decide the future of the world in any direction, and they did, by creating the Nation of Israel.

In essence, the greatest conspiracy is today found in our history books, that systematically portray nations as powerful. That is certainly not the case, in a world controlled by the Banking System. Armies and alliances can't be obtained without financial support, which is to say, a decision made by the Rothschild Family.

The Rothschild financed some of the greatest wars in Europe by aiding Napoleon Bonaparte and Hitler, among others. In fact, Gutle Rothschild, was quoted saying: "If my sons did not want wars, there would be none."

THE SECRET EMPIRE: THE HIDDEN TRUTH BEHIND THE POWER ELITE AND THE KNIGHTS OF THE NEW WORLD ORDER

The Business Insider, said that, "The Rothschilds are the most famous banking family in history. In the 19th century they lent money to Kings and governments and funded both sides in the Napoleonic wars. And they once saved the Bank of England from collapse with their own money" (In Business Insider).

It is then with no surprise that the Rothschild have been accused of everything from deliberately starting wars, to assassinating presidents and controlling the entire global financial system.

Mayer Amschel Rothschild, founder of the Rothschild banking dynasty, and referred to as the founding father of international finance (by Wikipedia), as well as one of the most influential businessmen of all time, according Forbes Magazine, said it himself:

"Permit me to issue and control the money of a nation, and I care not who makes its laws!"

Chapter 25: The Empire of the Rothschild.

During the 19th century, the Rothschild family possessed the largest private fortune in the world, as well as in modern world history.

Prior to centralized banking, each commercial bank in the United States issued its own notes. By creating the US Federal Reserve — a private banking system — the Rothschild were able to monopolize the US economy and, by default, associate it with England.

President Woodrow Wilson, through the Reserve Act, allowed The Federal Reserve to transform the United States into a corporation of the Rothschild.

When the Federal Reserve Act was passed, the Constitution ceased to be the governing covenant of the American people, and the country was handed over to a small group of international bankers controlled by the Rothschild through London.

Each of the twelve Federal Reserve Banks is organized into a corporation whose shares are sold to the commercial banks and thrifts operating within the Bank's district. Shareholders elect six of the nine the board of directors for their regional Federal Reserve Bank as well as its president.

Eustace Clarence Mullins and Gary Kah, have showed in their books, that many of these banks are owned by about a dozen European banking organizations, mostly British, and most notably belonging to the Rothschild banking dynasty.

Through their American agents, they are able to select the board of directors for the New York Fed and to direct U.S. monetary policy. And so, "The most powerful men in the United States were themselves answerable to another power, a foreign power, and a power which had been steadfastly seeking to extend its control over the young republic since its very inception. This power was the financial power of England, centered in the London Branch of the

House of Rothschild. The fact was that in 1910, the United States was for all practical purposes being ruled from England, and so it is today" (Eustace Mullins).

According to the FED Board's 1995 Annual Report, the System had a net income totaling $23.9 billion, which, if it were a single firm, would qualify it as one of the most profitable companies in the world. Nearly all of the Fed's annual profits are paid to the federal government. And accordingly, a lion's share of $23.4 billion, which represents 97.9% of the Federal Reserve's net income, was transferred to the Treasury. The Federal Reserve Banks kept $283 million, and the remaining $231 million was paid to its stockholders as dividends.

Today, the use of the dollar as an exchange currency in the world's economy and the Commonwealth of Nations (formerly known as British Commonwealth) with the City of London (Rothschild State) as the Headquarters, are both part of the strategy of the Rothschild family, and which allowed them to secure the British Empire as the world's most influential until now. And yet, the Rothschilds have been and still are involved in many scandals and lawsuits related to money laundering.

The Commonwealth of Nations, is a political association of 54 member states, all of which are under the control of the Rothschild Family.

Chapter 26: How Souls Are Bought and Possessed.

Everyone who has an ego is vulnerable to the influence of greed and sin, through a predisposition for arrogance. And this is the channel by which a soul can be corrupted and demonically possessed.

We see this predisposition in politics, as much as in religion, and in any religious group. As soon as someone falls into the trap of thinking that his religion is superior to others, this person is already vulnerable to any form of manipulation, either psychological or financial.

Praying daily with a holy book won't make any difference at that point. Because the act of trusting blindly in those who are part of our group while rejecting outsiders, is already a demonstration of lack of empathy and a willingness for manipulation.

In order for someone to become demonically possessed, this person has to simply lose the sense of empathy for the suffering of others, which occurs when associating with a group of people that he considers to be above others. That's how a mental predisposition for narcissism, psychopathy and sadism appear.

Many experts, including psychiatrist Morgan Scott Peck, believed in this association and wrote several books about it.

According to Dr. Peck, "Since narcissists deep down, feel themselves to be faultless, it is inevitable that when they are in conflict with the world they will invariably perceive the conflict as the world's fault. Since they must deny their own badness, they must perceive others as bad. They project their own evil onto the world. They never think of themselves as evil, on the other hand, they consequently see much evil in others."

Such demonic control occurs now through the banking system, because this is the easiest path for the corruption of the human mind. Through the banking system, is possible to either support or withdraw help from any organization, institution or religious group, and even country.

However, this is a control made at the top of the hierarchy. At the bottom of the social hierarchy, the control is applied through the fear of death and the need for survival. In other words, this control is made through a political manipulation, using a combination of mass unemployment and basic income (fear of starvation).

Many revolutions where engineered through this mass manipulation, and many Communist regimes and Fascist governments took power following moments of despair in the population. The Nazi Party, for example, received the support of a starving and impoverished Germany.

This control can also be achieved, for example, through the use of a bioweapon, like COVID-19, because it allows doing both things: create the fear of death in one end, and the fear of unemployment and starvation in another.

The complete dependency and obedience of the masses during a pandemic, automatically gives a totalitarian power to their government. A power which infatuates the ego of the leaders, and that they won't want to let go easily, but are more likely to keep and abuse.

Chapter 27: Satanic Rituals and Human Sacrifices.

There is no division between politics, bankers and religion any longer. But Satanism or demonic possession, along with psychopathy and narcissism, are also not speculations or metaphysical evidences, as blood rituals and sacrifices to Lucifer are indeed practiced throughout the world.

This was clearly exposed by a dutch banker named Ronald Bernard, who also said that, "As long as people don't realize how it works, how they're deceived... how they're being robbed... how their value is taken away from them to enrich the rich even further... as long as the people don't see this, as long as they are not aware, nothing will change...Everything you want to know about the world, you can know by following the money".

Bernard continued, saying that those at the top look down upon ordinary humans and laugh at their misery. When referring to his own experiences, he said:

"We looked down on people — mocked them. They were just a product. Waste! Everyone and everything was worthless trash! Nature, the planet, everything could burn and break. Just useless parasites."

The desensitizing through human sacrifice, orgies and other degrading habits, was part of a process, as he described, needed to create a ruthless but obedient class of bankers, who would go on to obey the influence of the Rothschild family.

Psychologists have systematically observed that narcissists are not born this way but traumatized enough to make a drastic choice. They become narcissistic as a decision to separate themselves from empathy, and also their own emotional suffering. This situation, on the other hand, reinforces the demonic power over their mind. Basically, narcissists create narcissists, which is the same as to say that demonic possession reinforces itself through the weakest souls and by weakening them as well.

The narcissist then becoming demonically possessed, becomes a totally different entity — can't be changed, can't be contradicted, and can't be confronted. And is obsessed with the destruction of anything that exposes him or her to the light of truth, while hating compassion and despising love — both conditions that lead to introspection.

The narcissist becomes a demon in disguise. And this is very likely the reason as to why the Satanic rituals intend to shock and cause trauma. The practice reinforces the mental pressure and trauma towards facilitating demonic possession among those who participate in it.

The so called snuff rituals, for example, in which a person is tortured to death, are also so shocking that one needs to necessarily shutdown his emotions and sense of empathy to be able to handle witnessing such horrors.

In 1995, during a conference in Dallas, Ted Gunderson (former head of the FBI) warned about the proliferation of secret occultist groups, and the danger posed by the New World Order — an alleged shadow government that would be controlling the United States government. He also claimed that a "slave auction" in which children were sold by Saudi Arabian agents to wealthy men, had been held in Las Vegas; and that four thousand ritual human sacrifices are performed in New York City every year.

Gunderson believed that, in the United States, there is a secret widespread network of groups who kidnap children and infants, and then subject them to ritual abuse and subsequent human sacrifice. And yet, the idea among the masses that such traumas only occur in certain rituals is also very deceptive, because all horror movies, or action movies related to fights, murder and rivalry, have the same purpose — the desensitizing of the human mind, to diminish the levels of empathy among people, and then make demonic possession easier to occur.

Chapter 28: Narcissism and Demonic Possession.

A large amount of people are demonically possessed without knowing it. Every single person who engages in a mental conversation with herself, and is led to decisions based on such inner dialogues, is most likely possessed.

Such habit, nevertheless, is so common, that most people think it is normal. The abnormal is now seen as the new normal. The retarded, unable to rationalize their own actions, as well as the demonically possessed, with filthy thoughts, are the new mainstream.

Demonic possession always occurs through fear, lack of empathy and hatred. These emotions facilitate what we call inner conversations, and which the majority considers to occur between themselves — as in opposing two thoughts inside our own mind.

Actually, this is often occurring telepathically between our own mind and a demon — a demonic spirit or negative entity outside the physical form.

The process has been clearly explained by many credible sources, namely, Ann Barnhardt and Malachi Martin.

In his book, "Hostage to the Devil", the priest and exorcist Malachi Martin, details how possession is always gradual and happens through inner conversations.

There was, however, an attempt in the Psychiatric community to distinguish Malignant Narcissism from other types of narcissism, such as Covert Narcissism. But that's just another sign of the human tendency to explain that which people can't understand. For all forms of narcissism are demonstrations, at different levels, of a demonically possessed soul.

I have spent my entire life encountering such souls and that's how I know. Again and again, Lucifer sent to me the most beautiful women to seduce me and stop me from writing books. And what I did, that caused the most hatred and vicious attacks from these women, was actually and only writing books. They always attacked me the most during such moments, as if they knew I was writing something important. The dramas seemed to always appear in a precise timing.

I also noticed the coincidence when such girlfriends would insult me with topics related to what I was writing, even though they couldn't possibly know, as I never discussed the content of my work with them, not until it was already published. But there are no such things as coincidences, even if it is hard to believe. And yet, the vast majority of the people is too childish, ignorant and naive to admit the obvious in front of their eyes.

Most christians have possessed souls too among them but blind themselves by their arrogance and delusional idea that their members are all soldiers of christ. And the same occurs with all the other groups I have encountered. They assume that everyone in the group is perfect and superior to anyone else outside the group.

This is precisely what makes these groups subject to demonic possession. Satan loves arrogance! It makes everything easier! Because as soon as a human becomes arrogant, he or she also disconnects from the Main Source — God.

Demons are everywhere. I have seen demonically possessed souls praying to God, and it has been one of the weirdest experiences of my entire existence.

Our fight today occurs at truly many levels. There is corruption inside religion, and the truth is hidden from the public by mainstream media as well as social media, the politicians are easily corrupted, and most people are either too stupid, too ignorant, too scared or too naive to see the truth for themselves.

Chapter 29: The Branches of Neo-Occultism.

The United States of America, was supposed to be a free country and a save haven for those who escape religious persecution around the world. It attracted Protestants, Jews, and many other christian and religious minorities. But this religious freedom also made it a save haven for occultists, witches, satanists and, practically, any type of religious ideology, including the most absurd and illogical.

This freedom was legalized to promote a fertile ground for an alchemical process between all groups, leading to what the founders — freemasons and believers in freedom — saw as true enlightenment.

Such vision is well exposed in the Bill of Rights, under the first and fourth amendments:

- Freedom of religion, speech, press, assembly, and petition.

- Freedom from unreasonable searches and seizures.

And most importantly, the third and seventh amendments:

- Right to keep and bear arms in order to maintain a well regulated militia.

- Right of trial by jury in civil cases.

What makes these four amendments particularly important, is that they allow forming religious communities that are independent from a nationwide majority. In other words, they protect the people from having democracy used against themselves. Because, as Benjamin Franklin said: "Democracy is two wolves and a lamb voting on what to have for lunch, and liberty is a well-armed lamb contesting the vote."

There was a belief in individual freedom allowing those who seized the opportunity to create their own religion out of the analysis and investigation of others.

However, the knowledge and the possibilities are not separated things, and the authors of the Bill of Rights understood this, when creating these very important but also timeless rights.

It it precisely because of such legal protection, that the United States saw a huge expansion in the creation of new religious ideologies, and also the active participation of many people in those.

The search for answers and the investigative approach to religion is the true enlightenment-related process sought by the illuminists who were inspired both by Progagoras (in the idea that knowledge is relative to man) and Pythagoras (in the idea that the Creator can be understood through His Creations).

Such approach led to the reverence and prominence of many unusual individuals, who formed their own religion in the United States, namely:

- Anton Lavey — Founder of the Church of Satan;

- Aleister Crowley — Founder of the Ordo Templi Orientis;

- Joseph Smith — Founder of Mormonism;

- Lafayette Ron Hubbard — Founder of the Church of Scientology;

- Harvey Spencer Lewis — Founder of The Ancient Mystical Order Roase Crucis;

- Max Heindel — Founder of the Rosicrucian Followship;

- Charles Taze Russell — Founder of the Jehovah Witnesses.

These groups, as many others, no matter how similar or different, or even contradictory, they may seem between one another, are interconnected, either through their founders or their funding system.

THE SECRET EMPIRE: THE HIDDEN TRUTH BEHIND THE POWER ELITE AND THE KNIGHTS OF THE NEW WORLD ORDER

It is not a coincidence, for example, that The Church of Scientology, The Rosicrucian Fellowship of Max Heindel and the AMORC of Harvey Lewis, all have their headquarters in California and use the same symbols — Pyramids, Snakes and the Cross of Resurrection.

Chapter 30: The Truth about Scientology and Psychiatry.

Scientology may seem unique and well-organized, but Ron Hubbard didn't create anything new, just like the Freemasons and many others. Almost everything in Scientology, including what Scientologists call the "Emotional Tone Scale", was already known to the North American Rosicrucians and their ancestors — The European Rosicrucians. And was merely explored, analyzed through scientific or pseudo-scientific methods, simplified and extended by Ron Hubbard, for his own personal goals — which were initially the creation of a new science (and not a religion), reason why he chose the word Scientology to define it.

There is actually a double meaning in this word, as was the style of Ron Hubbard in everything he did, for Sci can mean both Scientific and Science Fiction. Both words which defined the founder — author of both scientific and sci-fi books.

He was covertly putting in front of his followers that Scientology is a half-science and half-fiction religion. But, somehow, people didn't seem to notice. Reason why it's also ridiculous to both discredit Scientology as a whole, and to follow it as a dogma.

To a great extent, Scientology is as true or false as Psychiatry, and the attacks from scientologists on Psychiatry, are basically a projection of their own limitations, for both are pseudo-sciences.

On the other hand, even though what Ron Hubbard did, was mostly a mixture of speculation and pseudo-science, the parts in Scientology that are indeed rooted in truth, are not exclusive to Scientology but taken from Rosicrucianism.

Ron Hubbard tried to hide this fact by referring to ancient traditions and attributing part of it to his visits to the lamaseries of Tibet, and listening to, and enquire, the Buddhist monks there. Events that were never proven to be true.

L. Ron Hubbard was a good liar, but we can't blame him for that. For it has always been a common practice among those who wanted to come out as original and attract a large following. Namely, Sigmund Freud, who gained the title of founder of Psychoanalysis, when Psychoanalysis is as old as the Hindu Vedic Texts.

Freud was a freemason, exploring religious beliefs through the lens of science, just like Hubbard did with Scientology. Freud was simply more successful than Hubbard in converting his followers to believers of his pseudo-science without the need to create a religion.

Since then, many researchers have proven that most of Freud's studies were actually falsified.

According to Allen Esterson, and David Livingstone Smith (In the book, "Hidden Conversations"), "Freud twice stated that he would be presenting the clinical evidence for his claims, but he never did so, which critics have argued means that his clinical claims have had to be taken largely on trust."

In other words, psychology and psychiatry are rooted on faith. They should be labeled Psychiatrism and Psychologism instead. They are as much of a science as Scientology is.

This truth has been confirmed by many psychiatrists, namely, Dr. Loren Mosher (Clinical Professor of Psychiatry, Chief of the Center for Studies of Schizophrenia in the National Institute of Mental Health, and member of the American Psychiatric Association). He said that, "The DSM — Diagnostic and Statistical Manual of Mental Disorders, is the fabrication upon which psychiatry seeks acceptance by medicine in general. Insiders know it is more a political than scientific document. Some take it seriously, others more realistically. It is the way to get paid. But there are no external validating criteria for psychiatric diagnoses. There is neither a blood test nor specific anatomic lesions for any major psychiatric disorder. Is psychiatry a hoax — as practiced today? Unfortunately, the answer is mostly yes."

THE SECRET EMPIRE: THE HIDDEN TRUTH BEHIND THE POWER ELITE AND THE KNIGHTS OF THE NEW WORLD ORDER

Dr. Peter Breggin, US Psychiatrist and author of many books on the subject of psychiatric fraud, went further to admit that, "There is a great deal of scientific evidence that stimulants cause brain damage with long-term use, yet there is no evidence that these mental illnesses exist. Despite more than two hundred years of intensive research, no commonly diagnosed psychiatric disorders have proven to be either genetic or biological in origin, including schizophrenia, major depression, manic-depressive disorder, the various anxiety disorders, and childhood disorders such as attention-deficit hyperactivity. At present there are no known biochemical imbalances in the brain of typical psychiatric patients — until they are given psychiatric drugs."

Dr. Joseph Glenmullen (US psychiatrist, and Professor at the Harvard University Medical School), confirmed the words of Dr. Peter Breggin, when saying that, "While there has been no shortage of alleged biochemical explanations for psychiatric conditions, not one has been proven. Quite the contrary. In every instance where such an imbalance was thought to have been found, it was later proven false."

In other words, and as Dr. Niall McLaren (Psychiatrist, and Former head of the Department of Psychiatry in the Repatriation Hospital of Australia) said, "Psychiatry is not science, it's pseudoscience,.. and the claim that 'mental disease is brain disease', is an ideological claim."

This makes psychiatry an ideologic system rooted only on belief and faith, like any other religion in the world. And because any religion needs a holy book, the "DSM has been described as a 'Bible' for the field", according to Thomas Insel (Former Director of the US National Institute of Mental Health — NIMH).

Chapter 31: The Illusion Between All Religions.

If people knew the truth, they wouldn't be in Freemasonry, Scientology, Rosicrucianism or any of their branches, but instead following the oldest system they could find. And that is why most of these societies distort their real history, providing the false idea to their members that they're much older than they seem to be or somehow exclusive and unique.

A closer look at their foundation will lead us to the shocking acknowledgment that many of the founders were actually good friends. Ron Hubbard — founder of Scientology — , for example, was a close friend and student of the famous Aleister Crowley, which founded a new Knights Templar Order — The Ordo Templi Orientis — and was a great influence in the foundation of the Satanic Church of Anton LaVey.

Less known are other groups, either older or newer, but that follow the exact same principles — formally organized in what is known as Christian Gnosticism. Even though, in many cases, they refuse to study or talk about Christ, or follow religious scriptures that aren't their own or the ones created by their founders.

Gnosticism means knowledge of the self — from the word Gnosis, meaning self-awareness or cognition — and, therefore, the word can indeed be applied for non-christian studies as well as scientific researches.

Despite the illusion cast upon the masses, reality is divided merely by terminologies, in order to make the transition between different areas of study or religions almost impossible, if ever possible, or at least easy to be discredited, ridiculed and ignored.

The use of words as a way to create exclusivity and hide the truth, is well-know for many thousands of years, and included in the structure of the bible as well. Each religion using it, will interpret the information form a different angle and at a different level.

In the modern world, we find this technique being used mostly to hide self-awareness. Because it is not indented that humans can awake from their trance but rather studied within such trance. In doing so, it is easier to control the masses and keep them from ever awakening. And yet, the studies do exist, stratified and divided in different branches. For example:

- Metacognition: Is a concept used in psychology and psychiatry to explain self-awareness, or the cognition of one's own behaviors;

- Ethics: Is a greek concept used to explain the philosophical understanding of human behavior in relation to its implications and effects on others;

- Resurrection: Is the christian term used to explain the rebirth of the soul under the understanding of religious morality;

- Gnosis: Includes both the christian and philosophical meanings, as a technical term to explain the study of the self from an ethical perspective;

- OT (Operating Thetan): Is the technical word used by scientologists to explain the act of knowing and be willing to cause effect over matter, energy, space and time, including the control of one's own thoughts.

All these perspectives are directed at the same aim: the understanding of the self.

For the common mortal, it is definitely difficult to understand what Christian Societies, Gnostic Orders and Satanic Groups all have in common, and that is why the masses will always be confused about the type of knowledge that these groups seek independently or how to use it, as they are in regards to the differences between good and evil, or faith and magic.

THE SECRET EMPIRE: THE HIDDEN TRUTH BEHIND THE POWER ELITE AND THE KNIGHTS OF THE NEW WORLD ORDER

Freemasons and Rosicrucians have as much in common as Christians and Satanists, Scientologists and Freezoners (also known as Free Scientologists), or Gnostics and Hindus, but only when the whole world reaches the spiritual level of being able to connect religious systems, will the human race finally find peace and enlightenment on Earth.

Maybe also by then, humanity will find the ultimate connection between science and religion. For as Nikola Tesla said, "The day science begins to study non-physical phenomena, it will make more progress in one decade than in all the previous centuries".

Chapter 32: The Hidden Truth in All Religions.

We haven't evolved in our understanding about spirituality or gained more knowledge about it. What we did was create more organizations and societies based on the exact same principles, so that everyone can be happy and worship or not whoever they want, while interpreting the same words in their own way.

The level of expansion is today such, that most of the schools of knowledge and religious studies won't see any link connecting them and won't want also, in many cases, use the same books.

The vast majority of the members in these societies don't know this, because, like anyone else, they're afraid to think for themselves, while blindly following their leaders and worshiping them like prophets of the only truth — the supreme truth above all other truths.

The One Truth remains difficult to understand for the majority of the population.

That is why the prophets come to the scene, as simply individuals that can interpret these books and end up creating their own following, either by founding their own society, writing books or doing public speakings. And, because they often face persecution and ridicule, they are also and usually forced to close their members in a secret society with special rituals, initiations and laws.

The use of abstraction and metaphysical interpretations has been, for these reasons, ways of shielding the truth from attackers.

That is why Rosicrucianism, as Hinduism and many other old religious traditions, are so difficult to interpret. It is also for this reason that Ron Hubbard created his own words within Scientology, as a form of codifying the whole religion to a level that makes it impossible for any outsider to understand anything about it, even when finding the religious books used by the members.

Abstraction has always been an efficient mechanism of defense to hide the truth from the public eye, while misleading the immoral or rejected. But many egotistical individuals neglected such facts when promoting themselves above the sacred secrets. And that, not only caused the decline of the societies, but also attracted the interest of the most diabolical.

Most gnostic schools focus on different things, and with a very unique interpretation about them, but while some societies are easier to understand, Rosicrucian writings and concepts, or even the oldest Gnostic manuscripts, are still quite far from the common mind to grasp. And most wouldn't even be able to understand anything without suitable help.

This difficulty is related to the fact that we don't understand this knowledge with our brain. Spiritual knowledge implies awareness and that's why these societies have hierarchies, branches, exercises or rituals of purification, and focus on a ladder or pyramid to a complete awakening, also known as freedom from the influences of the material world, or freedom in the art of masonry.

Chapter 33: The Spiritual and Sexual Perversions.

Spiritual freedom has been commonly known as enlightenment. But is actually a complex system of spiritual evolution.

Knowingly or unknowingly, members of secret societies train in the art of masonry — the art of rebuilding the soul. But the topic is complex and has been also confused with witchcraft and satanism, because it follows the same paradigm about control over the physical nature of existence.

These individuals see the world and humans in a very unique way, while "the majority are unable to see beneath the surface of the physical body and thus to perceive the true state of the thoughts and feelings of others" (Max Heindel, Rosicrucian Fellowship).

The expansion of the spiritual wisdom — while the masses are kept blindly worshipping gods — then caused many orders to reinterpret their gnostic philosophies in opposing directions, and that is why the Luciferian beliefs, sexual rituals and even human sacrifices emerged, seemingly, from the same branches and inspired by the same texts.

I would say that it is a tendency of the human nature to explore its limits, reason why even the most strict christians groups, such as the Jehovah Witnesses, can't escape this tendency.

Barbara Anderson was a member of the Jehovah's Witnesses and worked at the Watchtower's headquarters in Brooklyn, New York, where during her years there, she researched the movement's official history and wrote a number of articles for their religious magazine.

During this time there, she found that the organization has a confidentiality policy which requires Witnesses involved in any judicial case to only talk about it with the judicial committee, or otherwise remain silent. Consequently, she noticed that there are many cases of rape and sexual molestation inside the group that remain hidden and suppressed from the general public.

Most of these cases are related to child sexual abuse within the organization.

The Watch Tower Society — also known as the Jehovah Witnesses — has been, according to her research, settling child sexual abuse lawsuits out-of-court for many years, although quietly, secretly, one at a time.

In 2003, attorneys for dozens of plaintiffs publicly filed more than twenty child sexual abuse lawsuits against the group, mostly in California. But none of these lawsuits made it to open court. Quite a number of lawsuits were dropped by plaintiffs' attorneys, although in 2007, seven California cases, one Oregon case, and another in Texas, were settled out-of-court by the leaders of Jehovah's Witnesses for millions of dollars.

Chapter 34: How Greed Corrupted the World.

In the bible (Timothy 6:10), it says that, "The love of money is the root of all evil". But many have misinterpret this quote as if saying that money is evil, while in fact the "love of money" is here referring to greed. It is greed that has corrupted the entire world.

In the past centuries, we haven't witnessed only a war commanded by the Power Elite against the masses, but also a suppression of the knowledge available to change the world. For, at one point, it wasn't any more about religious secrets, but wealth, politics and world domination. And the dimension of this problem has increased beyond any reasonable, ethical or spiritual belief.

Corruption is now everywhere. And today, most of the people in power are nothing more than psychopaths with a tremendous political influence and greed with close to no limitations.

Hitler was aware of this corruption, and therefore, despite being a believer in the cause of the Teutonic Knights, was against Freemasonry. In his book, Mein Kampf, Hitler wrote that, "The general pacifistic paralysis of the national instinct of self-preservation begun by Freemasonry".

Hermann Göring, a leading member of the Nazi Party, reaffirmed that belief, saying that, "In National Socialist Germany, there is no place for Freemasonry".

The number of freemasons from nazi occupied countries who were murdered in concentration camps, is estimated to be around 200,000. But Freemasonry was also persecuted in nearly every communist country around the world.

The rivalry, however, is easily forgotten when there is an agenda to be followed. And this is why there was such a thing as project paperclip — a program used to recruit the scientists of Nazi Germany for employment in the United States — in order to continue the scientific researches of the nazis in the United States.

The Rothschild family was also able to negotiate with Hitler the shipping of the jews to Palestine, in order to create the State of Israel.

The jews entered as refugees and became the oppressors of the people who welcomed them. They colonized an entire territory by force and murdered many Palestinians in the process.

On the other hand, while historical events could make us believe that there is an opposition between Freemasonry and the beliefs of the christians, most of the modern and extremist Christian Societies, such as the Jehovah Witnesses and Mormonism, were founded by Freemasons.

While these things occur, an order claiming direct lineage from the Knights Templar (The Sovereign Magistral Order of the Temple of Solomon) says, in regarding to Freemasonry, that, "It's only connection to Masonry is one single isolated event of transient history, solely the fact that the Freemasonry movement was created in Scotland (in the 15th century) as a limited offshoot of a regional sub-group flowing from the 12th century Knights Templar. Ever since that brief moment in history, Masonry has evolved independently in its own direction, and has no affiliation with the modern continuation of the original Templar Order. Such Masonic "Knights Templar" are not Solomonic Templars: They are exclusively Masons, defined solely by their own separate (and very different) traditions and beliefs. Some genuine and important (but limited) Templar knowledge had been transferred to the Masons, and they subsequently used that for their own purposes at their own discretion".

The controversy doesn't end here though, as in 2008 another order, also claiming lineage from the Templars, the Association of the Sovereign Order of the Temple of Christ, decided to sue the Vatican in $150 billion for assets seized by the Catholic Church in 1307.

Chapter 35: The Committee of 300

In 2016, a list of members of the Secret Society known as 'Committee Of 300', was released by an insider.

According to him, these are what the masses call the Illuminati or Power Elite.

Dr. John Coleman said, in a public presentation that, "The Committee of 300 evolved out of the British East India Company's Council of 300 which was founded in 1727 by the British royal family. For decades the British East India and Dutch East India Companies amassed fortunes from their opium trade with China and now through the Committee of 300 they continue to wage phony drug wars around the world today".

Is is believed that all the powers on the planet are now united under this organization, which combines the monarchies, the bankers and many knights in positions of power.

Many believe that the leader is the Queen of England — Queen Elizabeth II, but according to everything mentioned and proven in this book, we know that the leader is in fact the Jesuit Pope Francis.

This truth matches the prophecy of Saint Malachi, in "The Prophecy of the Popes", that through a series of quotes, pointed exactly at this pope as being the last one.

The list has been divided in groups, to help in contextualizing the information previously presented in the book, although it is believed that many of the members, at the present moment, may not be the same.

1st Level of the Pyramid — Clergy

1. The Pope — Pope Francis

2nd Level of the Pyramid — Treasury

1. Rothschild, Jacob (Baron)

2. Rothschild, Evelyn Robert
3. Rothschild, Leopold David
4. Rothschild, David René James
5. Rothschild, Benjamin

3rd Level of the Pyramid — Global Management

1. Rockefeller, David Jr.
2. Rockefeller, David Sr.
3. Rockefeller, Nicholas

4th Level of the Pyramid — Monarchy

1. Margrethe II (Queen of Denmark)
2. Harald V (King of Norway)
3. Gustaf, Carl XVI (King of Sweden)
4. Beatrix (Queen of the Netherlands)
5. Carlos, Juan (King of Spain)
6. Sofía (Queen of Spain)
7. Abdullah II of Jordan (King of Jordan)
8. Albert II of Belgium (King of the Belgians)
9. Constantine II Greece (former King of Greece)
10. Simeon of Saxe-Coburg and Gotha (former King of Bulgaria)
11. Michael (King of Romania)
12. George, Charles Philip Arthur(Prince of Wales)
13. Emanuele, Vittorio (Prince of Naples, Crown Prince of Italy)
14. August, Ernst (Prince of Hanover)
15. Leka (Prince of Albania)
16. Alexander (Prince of Yugoslavia)
17. William (Prince of Wales)
18. Hans-Adam II (Prince of Liechtenstein)
19. Alexandra (Princess)
20. Massimo, Stefano (Prince of Roccasecca Dei Volsci)
21. Moritz (Prince of Hesse-Kassel)
22. Friedrich, Georg (Prince of Prussia)

THE SECRET EMPIRE: THE HIDDEN TRUTH BEHIND THE POWER ELITE AND THE KNIGHTS OF THE NEW WORLD ORDER

23. Willem-Alexander (Prince of Orange)
24. Philip (Prince, Duke of Edinburgh)
25. Christoph (Prince of Schleswig-Holstein)
26. Richard (Prince, Duke of Gloucester)
27. Colonna, Marcantonio (Prince and Duke of Paliano)
28. Constantijn (Prince of the Netherlands)
29. Ruspoli, Francesco (Prince of Cerveteri)
30. Mabel (Princess) of Orange-Nassau
31. Fabrizio Massimo-Brancaccio (Prince di Arsoli)
32. Friso (Prince) of Orange-Nassau
33. Anne (Princess Royal)
34. Edward (Prince, Earl of Wessex)
35. Michael (Prince) of Kent
36. Prince Lorenz of Belgium (Archduke of Austria-Este)
37. Sigismund (Archduke of Tuscany)
38. Margherita (Archduchess of Austria-Este)
39. Vladimirovna, Maria (Grand Duchess of Russia)
40. Henri (Grand Duke of Luxembourg)
41. Edward, Andrew Albert Christian (Duke of York)
42. Pio, Dom Duarte (Duke of Braganza)
43. Alphonse, Louis (Duke of Anjou)
44. Edward (Duke of Kent)
45. Borwin (Duke of Mecklenburg)
46. Grosvenor, Gerald (Duke of Westminster)
47. Franz (Duke of Bavaria)
48. Camilla (Duchess of Cornwall)
49. Carlos (Duke of Parma)
50. Camilla (Duchess of Cornwall)
51. Carlos (Duke of Parma)
52. Astor, William Waldorf (Viscount)
53. Williams, Shirley – Baroness Williams of Crosby
54. Wilson, David – Baron Wilson of Tillyorn
55. Levy, Michael (Baron)
56. Levene, Peter – Baron Levene of Portsoken
57. Carington, Peter (Baron Carrington)

58. Sassoon, James Meyer (Baron Sassoon)
59. Stevenson, Dennis (Baron Stevenson of Coddenham)
60. Woolf, Harry (Baron)
61. Ogilvy, David (13th Earl of Airlie)

5th Level of the Pyramid — British Knights

1. Worcester, Sir Robert Milton
2. Walker, Sir David Alan
3. Hampton, Sir Philip Roy
4. Sawers, Sir Robert John
5. Davies, Sir Howard
6. Craven, Sir John
7. Rifkind, Sir Malcolm Leslie
8. Castell, Sir William
9. Parker, Sir John
10. Bischoff, Sir Winfried Franz Wilhen "Win"
11. Manning, Sir David Geoffrey
12. Ritblat, Sir John

6th Level of the Pyramid — Other Knights

1. Barroso, José Manuel
2. Blair, Tony
3. Clinton, Bill
4. Kissinger, Henry
5. Kerry, John Forbes (American politician)
6. Abramovich, Roman Arkadyevich (Israeli-Russian businessman)
7. King, Mervyn (British economist)
8. Ackermann, Josef (Swiss banker)
9. Kinnock, Glenys
10. Adeane, Edward
11. Agius, Marcus Ambrose Paul
12. Knight, Malcolm
13. Ahtisaari, Martti Oiva Kalevi

THE SECRET EMPIRE: THE HIDDEN TRUTH BEHIND THE POWER ELITE AND THE KNIGHTS OF THE NEW WORLD ORDER

14. Koon, William H. II
15. Akerson, Daniel
16. Krugman, Paul
17. Kufuor, John
18. Lajolo, Giovanni
19. Lake, Anthony
20. Lambert, Richard
21. Amato, Giuliano
22. Lamy, Pascal
23. Anderson, Carl A.
24. Landau, Jean-Pierre
25. Andreotti, Giulio
26. Laurence, Timothy James Hamilton
27. Leigh-Pemberton, James
28. Anstee, Nick
29. Leonard, Mark
30. Ash, Timothy Garton
31. Leviev, Lev
32. Levitt, Arthur
33. Aven, Pyotr
34. Balkenende, Jan Peter
35. Lieberman, Joe
36. Ballmer, Steve
37. Livingston, Ian
38. Balls, Ed
39. Loong, Lee Hsien
40. Louis-Dreyfus, Gérard
41. Belka, Marek
42. Bergsten, C. Fred
43. Mandelson, Peter Benjamin
44. Berlusconi, Silvio
45. Bernake, Ben
46. Bernstein, Nils
47. Martínez, Guillermo Ortiz
48. Berwick, Donald

49. Mashkevitch, Alexander
50. Bildt, Carl
51. McDonough, William Joseph
52. McLarty, Mack
53. Blankfein, Lloyd
54. Mersch, Yves
55. Blavatnik, Leonard
56. Bloomberg, Michael
57. Bolkestein, Frits
58. Miliband, David
59. Bolkiah, Hassanal
60. Miliband, Ed
61. Bonello, Michael C.
62. Mittal, Lakshmi
63. Bonino, Emma
64. Moreno, Glen
65. Boren, David L.
66. Murdoch, Rupert
67. Bronfman, Charles Rosner
68. Napoléon, Charles
69. Bronfman, Edgar Jr.
70. Nasser, Jacques
71. Bruton, John
72. Niblett, Robin
73. Brzezinski, Zbigniew
74. Nichols, Vincent
75. Budenberg, Robin
76. Nicolás, Adolfo
77. Buffet, Warren
78. Noyer, Christian
79. Bush, George HW
80. Ofer, Sammy
81. Cameron, David William Donald
82. Ollila, Jorma Jaakko
83. Cardoso, Fernando Henrique

THE SECRET EMPIRE: THE HIDDEN TRUTH BEHIND THE POWER ELITE AND THE KNIGHTS OF THE NEW WORLD ORDER

84. Oppenheimer, Nicky
85. Osborne, George
86. Oudea, Frederic
87. Carney, Mark J.
88. Patten, Chris
89. Carroll, Cynthia
90. Pébereau, Michel
91. Caruana, Jaime
92. Penny, Gareth
93. Peres, Shimon
94. Chan, Anson
95. Chan, Margaret
96. Chan, Norman
97. Pöhl, Karl Otto
98. Powell, Colin
99. Chartres, Richard
100. Prokhorov, Mikhail
101. Chiaie, Stefano Delle
102. Quaden, Guy Baron
103. Chipman, Dr John
104. Rasmussen, Anders Fogh
105. Chodiev, Patokh
106. Reuben, David
107. Cicchitto, Fabrizio
108. Reuben, Simon
109. Clark, Wesley Kanne Sr. (General)
110. Rhodes, William R. "Bill"
111. Clarke, Kenneth
112. Rice, Susan
113. Clegg, Nick
114. Cohen, Abby Joseph
115. Cohen, Ronald
116. Roach, Stephen S.
117. Cohn, Gary D.
118. Robinson, Mary

119. Cooksey, David
120. Rodríguez, Javier Echevarría
121. Cowen, Brian
122. Rogoff, Kenneth Saul "Ken"
123. Roth, Jean-Pierre
124. Crockett, Andrew
125. Sassoon, Isaac S.D.
126. Dadush, Uri
127. Rubenstein, David
128. D'Aloisio, Tony
129. Rubin, Robert
130. Darling, Alistair
131. Safra, Joseph
132. Davignon, Étienne
133. Safra, Moises
134. Davis, David
135. Sands, Peter A.
136. Sarkozy, Nicolas
137. Deiss, Joseph
138. Scardino, Marjorie
139. Deripaska, Oleg
140. Schwab, Klaus
141. Dobson, Michael
142. Schwarzenberg, Karel
143. Draghi, Mario
144. Schwarzman, Stephen A.
145. Du Plessis, Jan
146. Shapiro, Sidney
147. Dudley, William C.
148. Sheinwald, Nigel
149. Duisenberg, Wim
150. Snowe, Olympia
151. Elkann, John
152. Soros, George
153. Specter, Arlen

154. Feldstein, Martin Stuart "Marty"
155. Stern, Ernest
156. Festing, Matthew
157. Fillon, François
158. Steyer, Tom
159. Fischer, Heinz
160. Stiglitz, Joseph E.
161. Fischer, Joseph Martin
162. Strauss-Kahn, Dominique
163. Fischer, Stanley
164. Straw, Jack
165. FitzGerald, Niall
166. Sutherland, Peter
167. Tanner, Mary
168. Fridman, Mikhail
169. Tedeschi, Ettore Gotti
170. Thompson, Mark
171. Thomson, Dr. James A.
172. Tietmeyer, Hans
173. Geidt, Christopher
174. Trichet, Jean-Claude
175. Geithner, Timothy
176. Tucker, Paul
177. Gibson-Smith, Dr Chris
178. Van Rompuy, Herman
179. Gorbachev, Mikhail
180. Vélez, Álvaro Uribe
181. Gore, Al
182. Verplaetse, Alfons Vicomte
183. Gotlieb, Allan
184. Villiger, Kaspar
185. Green, Stephen
186. Greenspan, Alan
187. Volcker, Paul
188. Von Habsburg, Otto

189. Gurría, José Ángel
190. Waddaulah, Hassanal Bolkiah Mu'izzaddin
191. Hague, William
192. Wallenberg, Jacob
193. Walsh, John
194. Warburg, Max
195. Weber, Axel Alfred
196. Harper, Stephen
197. Weill, Michael David
198. Heisbourg, François
199. Wellink, Nout
200. Whitman, Marina von Neumann
201. Hildebrand, Philipp
202. Hills, Carla Anderson
203. Holbrooke, Richard
204. Williams, Dr Rowan
205. Honohan, Patrick
206. Howard, Alan
207. Ibragimov, Alijan
208. Wolfensohn, James David
209. Ingves, Stefan Nils Magnus
210. Wolin, Neal S.
211. Isaacson, Walter
212. Jacobs, Kenneth M.
213. Woolsey, R. James Jr.
214. Julius, DeAnne
215. Juncker, Jean-Claude
216. Wu, Sarah
217. Kenen, Peter
218. Zoellick, Robert Bruce

Also by Dan Desmarques

Spiritual Warfare: What You Need to Know About Overcoming Adversity
Collective Consciousness: How to Transcend Mass Consciousness and Become One With the Universe
The Spiritual Mechanics of Love: Secrets They Don't Want You to Know about Understanding and Processing Emotions
The 10 Laws of Transmutation: The Multidimensional Power of Your Subconscious Mind
The Evil Within: The Spiritual Battle in Your Mind
Deception: When Everything You Know about God is Wrong
How to Change the World: The Path of Global Ascension Through Consciousness
Religious Leadership: The 8 Rules Behind Successful Congregations
The 14 Karmic Laws of Love: How to Develop a Healthy and Conscious Relationship With Your Soulmate
A New Way of Being: How to Rewire Your Brain and Take Control of Your Life
Uma Nova Forma de Existir: Como Organizar Sua Mente e Assumir o Controle da Sua Vida
O Propósito da Sua Alma: A Reencarnação e o Espectro da Consciência na Evolução
Your Soul Purpose: Reincarnation and the Spectrum of Consciousness in Human Evolution
Encontre Seu fluxo: Como Adquirir a Sabedoria e o Conhecimento de Deus
Find Your Flow: How to Get Wisdom and Knowledge from God
66 Days to Change Your Life: 12 Steps to Effortlessly Remove Mental Blocks, Reprogram Your Brain and Become a Money Magnet
66 Dias Para Mudar Sua Vida: 12 Etapas Para Remover Bloqueios Mentais, Reprogramar Seu Cérebro e Atrair Dinheiro

Consciência Coletiva: Como Transcender a Consciência de Massa e Se Tornar Um com o Universo
Batalha Espiritual: O Que Você Precisa Saber Para Superar a Adversidade
Codex Illuminatus: Quotes & Sayings of Dan Desmarques
Codex Illuminatus: Citações e Provérbios de Dan Desmarques
As 14 Leis Cármicas do Amor: Como Desenvolver Um Relacionamento Saudável e Consciente Com Sua Alma Gêmea
The Hidden Language of God: How to Find a Balance Between Freedom and Responsibility
Your Full Potential: How to Overcome Fear and Solve Any Problem
The Secret Science of the Soul: How to Transcend Common Sense and Get What You Really Want From Life
?????????????????????
Technocracy: The New World Order of the Illuminati and The Battle Between Good and Evil
The Secret Empire: The Hidden Truth Behind the Power Elite and the Knights of the New World Order

About the Publisher

This book was published by 22Lions.com.
Follow us at Facebook.com/22lions